BLOOD-STAINED
VICTORY

BLOOD-STAINED
VICTORY

LISA BARNETT PRIDGEON

TATE PUBLISHING & *Enterprises*

Published by Tate Publishing & Enterprises, LLC
127 E. Trade Center Terrace | Mustang, Oklahoma 73064 USA
1.888.361.9473 | www.tatepublishing.com

Tate Publishing is committed to excellence in the publishing industry. The company reflects the philosophy established by the founders, based on Psalm 68:11,
"The Lord gave the word and great was the company of those who published it."

Book design copyright © 2011 by Tate Publishing, LLC. All rights reserved.
Cover design by Kenna Davis
Interior design by Joel Uber

Published in the United States of America

ISBN: 978-1-61777-241-2
1. Biography & Autobiography: Personal Memoirs
2. True Crime; General
11.08.30

DEDICATION

To Daddy, who stood beside me every step of the way. Daddy did not live to see me fulfill this dream, but I know within my heart I had his support. We often talked about one day putting my experience to paper to help reach young people. Daddy was a man that stood for honor and respect for God, country, and family. We children always knew when quitting time came, Daddy was coming home. I praise God for the security, love, and admiration we could see in Daddy's eyes and hear in his voice when he spoke.

To Rebekah Freimann Prudhomme, who I met when I was only eighteen and pursuing a higher education. Rebekah has listened to my dreams for twenty years. She has always supported and encouraged me to reach for the stars in life. Rebekah most importantly has stood for being a virtuous woman of God. Her relationship with the Lord has always inspired me. Rebekah and I have shared laughs that I will never forget. She has also let me cry on her shoulder a number of times. I praise God for our friendship; her friendship has been a cornerstone in my life.

Are you born again?

Daddy and me, 1987.

Daddy and me.

Daddy and Mother.

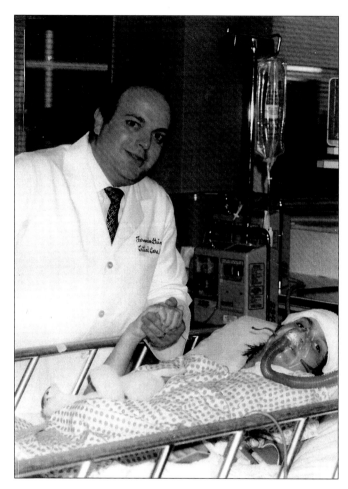

Doctor Stein and me.

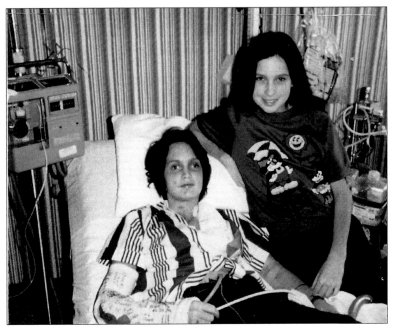

Jackie and me.

Lynne, Aunt Bernice, and me.

Mother

Rebekah and me.

The picture was taken 1985 at Easter Sunday
Left to right: Luke (Corey Hearon) Alex (Richard Barnett)
Lisa, Nelly (Sarah Barnett) Brittany (Rebecca Hearon)
There factious names are listed first which where used in the book.

Mother and me on my wedding day.

Jimmy and me on our wedding day.

FOREWORD

At a very young age, I realized Lisa was different. I was sixteen when she was born. The moment I saw her I was in love; my heart was captured. Growing up in a family of seven, born between two brothers, Lisa was the next-to-the-youngest. She was a tomboy plain and simple, yet as tender as she was rough. Lisa was the champion of the underdog on the school playground, the keeper of secrets to her classmates and siblings, and never met a stranger. She was a naïve farm girl, reared in a small country town. Her favorite pastime was playing basketball, running barefoot in the woods with her brothers, and playing with her niece and nephews. Lisa adored her family. The profoundness of her love and loyalty for family was obvious throughout her childhood. Most of all, Lisa had valor, determination to right a wrong, and great depths of courage and faith. It is those depths of courage and faith that would later assist in saving her life.

By the time Lisa was fourteen, her fame began to rise as being queen of the basketball court. She was gifted. Her tenacity caused her to be unafraid of the ball or opposite team players; she owned the ball court. She showed no signs of slowing down and becoming a proper young lady. At thirteen and fourteen, I would beg mother to make her brush her hair and put on a dress! That was a huge challenge. Lisa did not have time to worry herself with such trivial matters! So imagine our surprise when we learned an older boy was showing an interest in Lisa. Being the naïve person that she was, who always felt the need to rescue the down trodden, Lisa merely thought she had befriended a rejected boy on the school bus.

As Lisa was about to be shot that dark day, it was our beloved mother and brother whom she feared for most. Even during this ordeal, she was thinking of her family. Without her bravery, faith, and love for each of us, Lisa would have died. For four solid weeks, we were told every day that Lisa would not make it through the night. We will never know the amount of people who prayed for Lisa and our mother. People called from all over America telling us they had heard and were praying. Yes, prayers produced the miracle we needed for Lisa to survive. But without her blind faith and courage to endure the horrors she suffered in and out of the hospital, Lisa would not have lived. I also believe that Lisa hung on many times out of sheer love for our daddy, knowing how he would never get over losing her. Also, the fact that Lisa was an athlete in great shape, tough as a boot to be exact, greatly helped her fight the physical battle. She braved the terrors, fought tooth and nail to live, and believed her Lord God would not let her die. My precious sister is a faith fighter, a victor, and a woman who does not know the meaning of "can't." Her faith has only grown since those bleak hours, grown by leaps and bounds. For you see, Lisa knows what some of us only think; she knows for a fact that nothing is impossible with God and that He is true to His word, unable to go back on any of it! Therefore she knows first-handedly that she (and all of us) can do all things through Christ Jesus who strengthens her! I am proud to call Lisa my sister, my friend.

—Trisha Barnett-Hearon
This is her factitious name

TABLE OF CONTENTS

BLOOD SHED ON
HOLY GROUND

The shotgun blast echoed as the bullets ripped through Mother's right arm. It only took one shot to bring us to the mercy of God when it hit Mother's arm. Mother's blood, bones, and flesh flung into the air like a rural wind as I screamed "No!" One by one the pellets from the buckshot struck me in the face, right arm, right shoulder, chest, and neck. My body suddenly went limp. Blood began to gush from me. I fell to the cold, wet ground helpless, lying on my side. I felt like an animal that had been stalked and gunned down in the woods.

Through a blurry eye I noticed that Devin, my attacker, had stepped around Mother so he could get a good look at me. I lay motionless on the ground, praying that he would think I was dead. He stared at me with his cold, blue eyes, satisfied that I was now dead. He slowly turned and walked to his truck; nothing could stop him. Was he now past any feeling?

The sun rose as usual that Sunday morning deep in the heart of East Texas. The cold wind blustered across the brown grass as our family ate breakfast. It was time to get ready for church and Sunday school. Mother was determined to make me look like a young lady instead of a tomboy, which *I* preferred. My school friend, Carla Moody, had given me a curling iron as a Christmas present. Now on January 5, 1986, my mother intended to use that gift on my hair that morning. It didn't matter whether I liked it or not.

All I cared about was wearing my new clothes and shoes that were given to me for Christmas.

Ben, my older brother, had already bathed and was dressing in his room, listening to music playing on his radio. Alex, my younger brother, and I had taken our baths the night before. Now it was time for all of us to get dressed. Each of us wanted to look our best, but keep our individual styles. Daddy decided that since his back was hurting, he and Alex were going to skip Sunday school and only attend church. He told Mother to go ahead with Ben and me, and he and Alex would follow later. Ben, being the one in the spotlight, a big sixteen-year-old with his driving permit, wanted to drive us in the red four-door Chevrolet. Alex and I looked up to Ben, who we often took advice from when it came to a question of right and wrong. Mother was now dressed and wearing the pin I had bought her years ago at Wal-Mart. This special pin was in a heart shape that read "Mother" across it. As I feared, she called me to the dresser in my room. I did not want stupid curls in my hair. I wanted my hair to lie flat. Mother chided me that I did not have a choice in the matter. In short, I was going to mind her and allow her to style my hair. I wanted Mother to respect me for the person I was, and besides, I hated those stupid curls.

They just weren't my style. Mother insisted, telling me that she knew what was best for me. Besides, after I had seen them, and everyone complimented me at church, surely I would like them.

Very soon, it was time to leave. While walking to the car, I glanced at my sister's house, and I spied her peeking out her window. Candy, my older sister, was now living in the old camp house that Daddy had moved from the back twenty-five acres to the front near our house. Daddy and I, with the help from my other siblings, had remodeled it for her use. Candy was waiting for us to leave for church so she could come up to the house and prepare breakfast.

By now the fog we'd had earlier that morning had lifted, but the ground was still soaking wet from the heavy dew and rain the night before. We drove down our red, muddy, dirt road as Mother and Ben, sitting in the front seat, began talking to each other. As for me, I just sat in the back seat with arms folded with a look on my face. I would have to forgive Mother for curling my hair against my wishes, but that wasn't going to happen anytime soon. I was trying my best to find a way to make it go flat without using my hands, since Mother had told me to keep my hands off the curls.

We had just turned off our dirt road and began climbing what we called "the hill" on Scrapping Valley paved road. As we reached the top of the hill, Mother exclaimed, "Ben, be careful. Here comes a drunk driver." Ben slowed down to prevent an accident. I forgot all about being mad at Mother. I leaned over between the two seats to get a better view.

The approaching truck sped faster toward us. Suddenly we recognized the driver. "Oh no, it's Devin!" Mother yelled, "Ben, get off the road, or he is going to hit us!"

No more than mere inches separated Devin's truck from the front of our car. Ben steered our car as best he could, but it began to sink in the muddy ditch. I quickly turned around so as to see what Devin would do next. As I feared, Devin turned his truck around with a fast U-turn at the bottom of the hill. Mud and dirt flew up in the air as he came after us again.

I began gasping for breath as panic began to flood my veins like a tidal wave. Ben had now maneuvered our car back on the roadway. I yelled, "He's coming! He's coming! Devin turned around. He's coming to kill me. What are we going to do?"

Mother looked into my eyes and without hesitation said, "Let's pray for the angels to come!" Then she instructed Ben, "Give it all she's got! Go as fast as you can! Put it to the floor! But be careful to stay on the road. If you run off again, he will ram us into a tree!" I did as Mother said and tried to pray as best as I could, but prayer seemed to be useless at this point. I wiped away my tears as terror began to grasp me in my innermost being. Quickly, Devin caught up with us. He was staring at me even as I cried out to my heavenly Father. I peered out the back window, and at that moment, I saw the demons raging in his eyes; I knew it was over for me.

There would be no more talks, visits, laughs, excitement, or loving moments. Those things that we had shared were gone. Instead, the deadly truth was right beside him. Propped up on his truck's floor board was his .12-gauge shotgun, resting near his broad shoulders. This was a gun that had family pride and respect behind it. Now, this gun was fully loaded. Looking at the gun, I felt deep within my soul that my worst fear was coming true—that he had come after me with the intent to kill! There was a full box of shells on the dash, just in case he needed them to finish the job he had come to do. Mother told Ben to start blowing the car horn and perhaps Billy Don Sparks, a local town deputy who lived nearby, would be home and notice that we needed his help immediately as we raced past.

As we sped past the few homes on Scraping Valley Road, no one appeared to be stirring. There was no one to see that we were fleeing for our lives. We had traveled about two miles when the Macedonia Baptist Church came into view. The congregation was gathering for Sunday School and church. Mother and Ben decided if we stopped there, surely Devin would pass on by. Here we would have many witnesses. Ben drove the car right up to a big oak tree that stood in the grassed-over parking lot.

Devin did not pass by as we had hoped. He followed us into the parking lot. He jumped out of his truck, holding his shotgun. He ran up to our car and pointed the gun directly at me. Tears streaming down my face, I ducked down to avoid a direct shot through the window. "This is the last time ya'll are going to do this to me!" Devin yelled. "This is the last time ya'll are going to do this to me! Lisa, I am going to kill you! I am going to kill you! Get out of the car. I am going to blow your head off! You will never do this to me again! I am going to kill you!"

"Mother, I will take care of this, just stay in the car," Ben said as he opened his car door. "Devin, Devin, look, we are not going anywhere! Look, I will turn the engine off. Just put your gun down. Devin, we can talk about this. We don't have to settle it with guns!"

I kept moving around in the back seat, like an animal, doing my best not to give Devin a direct shot. Terror raced through my body as I screamed and cried out to my Lord and Savior. "Dear God, save my weary soul. Oh my God, please let him leave before Daddy drives up. Oh Lord, I am sorry, but I don't want to die. Help me!" My life flashed before my eyes. Devin was pointing the gun toward me. Ben continued to try to get Devin's attention. He assured Devin that he would turn the car off so we could all talk.

Brother Clarence Howell, the pastor of the church, assisted his daughter Mary, who had cerebral palsy, into the church, then came back out and tried to reason with Devin. He kept saying, "Please, Devin, don't shoot. Please, Devin, don't shoot!"

Mother decided that Devin was listening to no one, so after kicking open her car door and getting out to face Devin, she decided to take matters into her own hands. Mother looked right down the gun barrel as marched directly toward Devin. Bravely, she managed to back Devin all the way back to the door of his truck.. She ordered him, "In the name of the Lord, put the gun down."

Ben walked away from the car and now was beside the truck. His hastily devised plan was to jump Devin from the side. Brother Howell was directly behind Mother, still pleading with Devin not to shoot anyone and to put the gun away. The rest of the congregation was standing twenty to thirty feet away, all pleading for Devin not to shoot anyone. I huddled on the floorboard of the car. *What would happen if Daddy drove up?* I knew deep inside my inner being, that Devin was not going to leave the church house until he thought I was dead. I feared that my brother, Ben, or Mother would get killed trying to protect me. Every muscle in my body was shaking as I reached over and opened the car door. Crawling out on the wet, cold ground, I screamed at the top of my lungs. But no one seemed to hear my cry. I kept screaming, "I am the one he wants! I am the one he wants!"

I remembered Mother's words: Pray unto the Lord. With my hands pressed together, I knelt, praying unto the Lord above to send guardian angels to save my life. Suddenly, Devin pointed his gun at Ben, who was about to attack him, and yelled, "If you move one more inch, I will kill you." Ben froze in his footsteps. Devin then pointed the gun back toward Mother and said, "I don't want to shoot you. But I will, if you don't get out of my way."

Mother took one more step of faith. Looking down the gun barrel, she said, "I said, in the name of Jesus, put that gun down."

Devin, amazingly, started lowering his gun, until he had it almost all the way down. Then, suddenly he jerked the gun back up and took aim at us. When Mother realized he was about to fire the gun, she cried out, "Dear God, send the angels!"

OUR LIVES HANGING
BY A THREAD

Although I could see only out of my right eye, I saw Devin get back into his truck and drive south on Highway 87 toward his house. Seeing this brought some relief to me, for now he was gone. Mother was screaming, "Oh my God, it hurts." Then she pleaded to the congregation, "Ya'll going to just let me stand here 'til I faint?" They were all frozen as the sound of the gun blast still echoed in their ears. Finally reality hit them, "Oh God, he shot them. He shot them!" They rushed to Mother's side to administer what first aid they could.

Her arm had been completely severed, except for one blood vessel and two pieces of skin connecting her arm right below her elbow.

David Ener, one of my cousins, was in the parking lot as the incident was unfolding. He fled to Austin's home to call the Sheriff's department. David had a crippled leg, but amazingly, he had walked so fast that he was on the phone with the Sheriff's department when he heard the gunshot. Although David eyes did not see the blood shed deep within his soul he knew as the sound wave came through the walls of the house. He began shouting on the phone "Send the ambulance they been shot. We need help! Send the ambulance now!"

I lay on the cold, wet ground, unable to cry for help, for I, too, had been hit. My vocal cords had been damaged. Blood was pouring from a half-dollar sized hole in my neck, which had left me helpless. Bullet after bullet had torn through my flesh, ripping into my esophagus and neck.

Everyone had raced to Mother to give her help. No one seemed to realize that the same shot that had brutally gone through Mother's arm had also pierced my body. I later found out that one of the bullets had traveled through my face all the way to my brain, limiting the vision in my left eye, but I could see people running around. I could hear my mother say, "No, I cannot lie on that wet ground, because I will get pneumonia."

Austin McElroy, one of Mother's cousins, lived right across the street from the church. Austin and some other people found a chair for Mother to sit in and some blankets to cover her. Austin applied a tourniquet in an attempt to save Mother's arm. When he would release the tie from around it, blood shot into the air like a spring of water. Mother was seated with Ben next to her in a state of shock. She looked at him and said, "Ben, go call our church, tell them what happened and to pray for us." He quickly turned and ran to the phone to call Pineland Life Teaching Center.

Sammy Cousins, one of the church congregation witnesses, after seeing that Mother was taken care of, finally looked my way and realized that I had been shot also. He ran to my side, knelt down and lifted me off the ground, and laid my battered body on his knees. Virginia Smith, another witness, ran to get blankets and coats to cover me. Sammy tried to keep me calm. He leaned over me and put his face close to mine. He told me that I was going to be okay because the ambulance was on the way. Fear, not for my life, but for my mother's life, began to grip me. I was lying in such a way that I could not see her. I was terrified that my mother was going to bleed to death. I had prayed for the Lord to save my life, but I didn't think to pray for Mother or Ben. I feared Mother would die and it would all be my fault. I began to fight, hoping I could crawl to her some way, but Sammy held me firmly in his arms, trying to keep me from hurting myself any worse. I lay in his arms unable to speak as blood gushed out of my mouth.

My heart cried out to my Lord and Savior. I was ready to give up the struggle and submit to death when I looked into the heavens. I saw the clouds open up and what I believed to be two warrior angels, with staffs in their hands, descending from heaven. I had to believe then that everything was going to be okay. I just wished so much I could help my mother. I then heard voices all around me. I fought with all my strength just to breathe. The bullets had hit both lungs, but the left lung had been hit the hardest and collapsed, making it practically impossible to breathe. Blood was gushing from my neck, around my vocal cords, through the hole the bullet had made. My right arm, which had caught multiple bullets from elbow to wrist, was shattered into pieces. My arm resembled like the pine splinters we used to start a fire. Lying on the ground, I wondered, *Is Daddy here yet? Where are Daddy and Alex?*

Daddy and Alex were standing on the front porch of the house when they heard the gunshot in the distance. They got in the truck not knowing what they were about to discover. Ben had returned from calling the church when he saw Daddy drive up in his truck. He ran into the road and flagged Daddy down to tell him the horrifying news. Daddy raced over to see Mother and me each in our own puddle of blood. He ran to my side and knelt on his knees. He said, "Lisa, hang in there. You are going to make it. The ambulance is on the way. Lisa, you're going to be okay. Daddy is here now. You are going to be okay."

Before I could even think of what I wanted to say to Daddy, he stood up and took charge of the situation. The sheriff had arrived, and Daddy, with tears streaming down his face, cried out, "Blan Greer, you better get him, or I will! Look what he did to my family!" I couldn't understand everything that was going on.

Alex, my younger brother, arrived, knelt down by my side, and said, "Lisa, hang in there; you're going to make it! You're going to be okay!" Looking into the crystal blue eyes of my twelve-year-old, blonde-haired brother, how could I doubt? I saw a tear coming out of the corner of one of Alex's eyes. It was as though a "what if" crossed his mind as he looked at me in silence for a few seconds. Then he took a deep breath, and with his well-known half smile said, "I love you." When I heard those words, all that mattered to me at the moment was my little brother's broken heart. I took in what air I could muster out of my collapsed left lung and injured right lung. I opened my mouth to say "I love you, too," to my little brother. Instead, when I opened my mouth as wide as possible, more blood poured out. Alex had handled all he could by my side, and he rose to his feet and walked away. I turned my head to watch him, when I saw Ben. I could not tell if he was hurt.

The next thing I knew, the ambulance had arrived. I was placed on the stretcher and lifted into the ambulance. I was trying to see Mother. Where was she? Everyone who had spoken to me had told me I was going to be okay, but no one had told me how Mother was doing. Much to my dismay, they placed Mother on my left side, my blind side. Fear began to tear at my insides. I was emotionally shredded at the mere thought of Mother leaving in a body bag. My mother! Was she going to lose her life attempting to protect me from Devin? *Oh dear God, all of this was my fault!*

Daddy had to make a tough decision. Should he go after Devin himself or trust the law to do their job? Ben and Alex were standing by Daddy's side with tears streaming down their faces. They were uninjured physically, but they were emotionally distraught. Daddy also knew that Candy was home alone. Would she be safe until Devin was apprehended? Daddy chose to trust the law as tears of anger, hurt, and despair streamed down his face.

Daddy asked Austin to take Alex and Ben to the home of Mr. and Mrs. Kent Hill, some friends of ours, until other arrangements for their care could be made.

Daddy hurried to his truck so he could follow behind the ambulance. It raced to Sabine County Hospital with Daddy following close behind. All the time he was thinking that our family was going to have to pull together and follow his lead.

One by one, our extended family was notified of the horrifying news. They all rushed to the hospital to be by Daddy's side. Candy and Carl, one of my older brothers, lived close enough to town that they were able to find Daddy at the hospital.

The hospital stood prepared for the emergency with Dr. Grover C. Winslow waiting for our arrival, even as the ambulance raced through town to the emergency room. Dr. Winslow examined both of us quickly. He determined that he needed to tend to mother first, else she might bleed to death.

Dr. Leonard Shockey arrived soon after we were put in emergency rooms one and two. He began the task of placing a trachea in my throat and hooking up an oxygen machine to my injured lungs. Dr. Winslow did all that he could do for Mother and ordered the ambulance driver to transport her on to Nacogdoches. He called ahead to speak with a Dr. Jorgensen personally. He explained that Mother was already handicapped in her left arm from a childhood injury. She needed this arm saved at all costs. He then assisted Dr. Shockey in preparing me for transport to Nacogdoches as well.

Daddy, struggling to comprehend what all had taken place, was joined by Candy and Carl in the waiting room as Mother was wheeled out of the ER to be transported to Nacogdoches. Daddy asked Carl to go in the ambulance with her. Daddy wanted to stay behind and ride with me. Candy and Daddy stood in the waiting room and prayed. They asked Almighty God to be with the doctors and nurses.

Sabine County Hospital contacted Joe Simmons, a Pineland volunteer firefighter and ambulance driver. They brought me outside when the ambulance was ready to transport me. The doctors quietly informed Daddy that I was in serious condition and that they should drive as fast as possible. Daddy sat down in the front seat of the ambulance as Joe radioed ahead, asking police officers to open up a right-of-way to Nacogdoches. Daddy kept looking back at me as I lay on the stretcher. I was unconscious and fighting to stay alive, and though I could not hear him, he kept repeating to me, "Hang in there. We are almost to the hospital."

As we entered Nacogdoches, the police were waiting at every red light, clearing the way for the ambulance through every intersection so we didn't have to stop until we arrived at the hospital.

BARNETTS GATHER
THE WAGONS

Mother was the first to come out of surgery and be placed in ICU. The hospital waiting room was beginning to fill up with family and loved ones who had heard about the shooting. My father stood at the ICU doors. He was anxiously waiting for information on how Mother and I were doing.

Tears of pain streamed down Daddy's face as family and friends arrived. Dr. Jorgensen was Mother's attending physician. He explained to Daddy and other family members that medically speaking, any arm needed two blood vessels to survive. Mother only had one blood vessel that survived the shooting, but due to Mother's left arm being handicapped already, they were going to do everything possible to save it despite the high odds against it.

Ron, my oldest brother, and his wife, Scarlet, soon arrived at the hospital. She lay in ICU with her arm in a sling, still in a state of shock from what had happened. Ron entered Mother's room and explained how she only had one good blood vessel. He spoke words of faith to Mother. He explained how God had allowed one blood vessel to survive the shooting so that the doctors could save her arm.

Dr. Donald Cagle, after hours in surgery on me, reported to my family on my condition. He explained how seriously injured I was and that I might not make it through the night.

My aunt Lavern, my mother's oldest sister, heard this report and said, "No, she is going to make it." She told the rest of the family standing around her that they had to pray! She went to an empty hospital room and fell on her hands and knees. She prayed that my life might be spared from this horrible crime of hate. My family and friends all prayed as I was rolled down a crowded hall to the Intensive Care Unit.

I lay in ICU unconscious from the surgery, my life completely in God's hands and at his mercy. The bullet was lodged in the left lobe of my brain, and the left lobe began to hemorrhage and swell while I was lying in the ICU. My left eye was completely swollen shut, and the rest of my face began to bulge out. My sinus cavities were exposed, and my neck was gaping open too, as though slashed with a butcher knife.

Caroline, my oldest sister, and her husband, Rex, rushed to the hospital. There they found a kind nurse who had been instructed to wait for their arrival. The nurse had tears in her eyes. Caroline knew that this was a life or death situation, despite how much Ron tried to convince her that it was not all that serious; her inner soul told her differently. She knew she had to pray for angels to come to minister healing through the hands of doctors. The kind nurse escorted Caroline through the crowd as Rex left to park the truck. There she met Daddy standing by the ICU doors. She rushed toward Daddy as the crowd stepped aside as father and oldest child's eyes met in a dark hour. He tried for a moment to hold back tears as he reached out to embrace Caroline. She looked into our Daddy's eyes and could see the pain and anguish. It was flowing like a river inside his heart. It seemed as though Daddy's eyes had faded to a lighter shade of blue, because of crying so many tears of hurt and despair. As she heard the report from Daddy, Caroline responded in faith. She believed that we, as a family, were going to pull through this. We were strong and all knew how to pray.

Devin, the shooter, was still at large. We tried to have faith in the justice system, but thoughts and fears of what he might do next gripped my family. At the same time, they tried their best to focus on giving their undivided attention and support to the recovery of Mother and me.

The power of the Lord was vibrating off the walls from different prayer groups in the waiting rooms. Nurses and even the busy doctors would stop and listen, stunned at such outpourings of faith. Everyone was doing their part whether on their knees or standing on their feet. The earnest cries for our lives to be spared echoed down the halls. The cord of the unconditional love of God spread throughout the hospital and bound everyone together. They vowed to stand against the attack of the enemy. Mother and I, though lying bed-ridden on our backs, could feel the prayers and love holding us up before our heavenly Father.

Mother was no longer fighting for her life. It was just a matter of saving her arm. I, on the other hand, lay fighting for every breath. To make things worse, I was aware deep in my subconscious thoughts that Devin was still a free man. The day passed by slowly and painfully, both emotionally and physically. Time had drifted into the wee hours of the night.

About ten that night, Daddy received word that Devin had been apprehended and was in jail. This brought a little relief to Daddy's mind. Devin was now where he could hurt no one else in our family. Then Daddy started worrying about something else. How could he go about making sure that Devin was not released on bail until the day of the trial? He knew in the depth of his heart that if Devin got out of jail, he might not be able to withstand the temptation of retaliating. Daddy spread the good news of Devin's capture to everyone in the family. Now they could sleep with a little more ease, knowing that Devin was behind barred doors, locked in a cell.

The first night finally dwindled into another day. I had undergone three major operations. Daddy had refused to leave the doors of ICU; weakness in his legs caused him to slide down to the floor. Family and friends stood helplessly in the hallways. The main battle that I seemed to be facing was severe respiratory distress. After a couple of days in ICU, I was returned to the operating room. The doctors hoped to find another airway to help me to breathe. They did extensive work on my trachea. Finally I was able to take some breaths on my own. I was then returned to the ICU, where I lay unconscious after the surgeries. The doctors told my family that as soon as I was stable, it would be best for me to be transported to Houston. Daddy stood like a military guard at the ICU doors. Daddy oversaw each visitor that had a brief moment to look into our eyes as we laid in ICU. Hours and hours passed; Daddy did not sleep or let a moment pass without crying out to our heavenly Father to intervene where doctors fell short. Finally Aunt Bernice insisted that a doctor give Daddy some medicine so he could sleep before he just completely collapsed on the floor. The doctor agreed and gave Daddy some medicine, and someone unknown to the family paid for a hospital room close to the ICU where Daddy finally laid his head to rest for a few hours.

Three days passed before I started communicating with the nurses. I wondered what was taking place. They brought me a clip board and a pen. I began writing to the best of my ability with my left hand. Carl, my older brother, had to read the hardest question. "Where is Devin?"

Carl reassured me over and over again, "Devin is in jail. You have nothing to be afraid of anymore." I asked so often that Carl quit answering me. Instead, he told me that I already knew the answer. He was the first one to begin testing my memory, despite my head injury and serious concussion. It got to the point that I could answer Carl when he would ask, "What did I tell you last time I was in here?"

My family and nurses did everything possible to keep my mind off of why I had been injured and focused more on my recovery. I was in a Nacogdoches hospital for seven days. The doctors were trying to stabilize my condition. Everyone was working hard to save my life. I, on the other hand, was deep in thought about the relationship that I had developed with Devin

MEMORIES OF YESTERDAYS

Despite my overwhelmingly strong medication, I remembered how Devin and I first became acquainted. I can't say that I honestly ever chose sides in our new neighborhood. I was only in the third grade when we moved from Magaso to Yellowpine. I was determined to be friends with everyone. I tried to always be the kid that spoke to the unloved. This community had far more roots and history than I could ever dare to grasp. Unfortunately, the families in this community seemed to let everyone know which side of the fence they were on. Every kid we met seemed to have certain other kids in the neighborhood that they would not play with. This was either by personal choice or by what their parents demanded.

It did not take us long to discover which kids in the neighborhood we would be hanging out with, whether it was riding horses, motorcycles, or go-carts to have fun. It seemed a lot easier to make friends in Magasco than it did in Yellowpine. In Yellowpine, there were more kids from different sides of the field. In Magasco, we were forced to get along because all our dads or mothers worked for the same company, United Gas Pipe Line. We even had a fenced-in station yard. There, anyone that lived in the white company houses could buy soft drinks for only twenty-five cents a bottle, plus all the ice out of the machine you wanted. We also had a pond in which we caught perch for trot-lining, a basketball goal in the circle, and an old tree house with a trolley in the woods. Every month the Magsco station yard would have a cook out. There was all the food one could eat, and we played hide-and-seek after our bellies were full. I loved finding Kathy Server, who always took the time to swing me from a tree in an old swing hanging from a low limb. At Magasco, it was much like living in a fantasy world. But, outside the fence, we had also made some friends. The kids all seemed to enjoy coming to our station yard and playing with us. Mother would let us leave the station yard to play with the neighborhood kids, too.

Jill Jackson, who was best friends with Candy, lived right outside the station yard. She was always real nice to Ben, Alex, and me, taking time to listen to us and watch us run and play. Mrs. Jackson would often let us come over and hang out with their family. When her grandchildren came from out of town, we really had a ball with them. They were indeed city kids. But after only a short time hanging out with us, they were soon climbing trees and howling as loudly as us.

I recall the day Ben threw a stick, fashioned like a spear, which accidentally hit Alison in the mouth, as she was sitting in a snake tree. Despite this accident, we kids all just "kissed and made up," so to speak. Ben got in trouble, and Alison got her wound stitched up. No grudge was held and "bygones were bygones."

But here in Yellowpine, neighbors all got along and helped each other. Daddy soon found out from neighbors, and from experience, that there was one family that didn't always play with a full deck of cards when it came to honesty. We would have stayed at Magasco, but the company broke up the station's yard. Then they sold the entire group of houses to company employees. My father, having already bought land in Yellowpine, chose to buy a company house. He then moved us to our new frontier.

It did not take Ben, Alex, and me long to start hanging out mostly with the James kids and Hill kids. They lived closer to our house and were more convenient to hang out with. And our parents had a lot in common. The James' children were named Sam and Stacy. The Hill's were named Neal and Tony. Neal and Sam were both older than Ben. But Tony was the same age as me and Stacy was the same age as Alex. I was only in third grade when we moved to Yellowpine, but I still attended school at Pineland.

For the most part, it was as though Devin didn't exist in my life at this time. I knew who he was from talk in the neighborhood, but for the most part, he was just an older boy that I never thought twice about.

It was amazing, lying in the hospital bed with all those machines hooked up to me, that in my mind I first thought about how pleasant life was before Devin became a factor. Daddy and Mother finally transferred Ben, Alex, and me to Hemphill school my fourth grade year. This was a big adjustment. It took me the next couple of years to truly feel like a Fighting Hornet and that I belonged at Hemphill School. I had finally made some friends who had helped me to fit into the groove of things.

Carla Moody, J.J. Michler, and Angie McDaniel had started showing me the ropes around campus. They inspired me to live a Godly life. We all came from Christian homes, but at school they knew how to live faithfully. Leo Winchester, who was Devin's younger brother, was in my class also. Thus I heard about Devin quite often when we all got together. We'd usually talk about things our older brothers and sisters did at home. But outside the classroom, Devin and I didn't hang out together. We hardly spoke when we rode home from school on the same bus.

In the hospital, I wondered just why Devin and I did begin crossing tracks. Before I could finish thinking about our first interactions, doctors came to my room with news I wasn't so happy to hear.

JOURNEY INTO
THE UNKNOWN

After a week in ICU, the doctors felt I was stable enough to be transported to a hospital in Houston. There they would have more specialized doctors to work on my injuries. When they told me this news, the first thought that raced through my weary mind was, what about Mother? Will Mother be transferred to Houston as well? Unfortunately, I was told that she would be staying in Nacogdoches with *her* doctors. Despite my mind being strongly medicated and still trying to grasp this dilemma, I without hesitation wrote on a clipboard: Can I see Mother to say goodbye, before I leave? Doctor Cagle reached out and squeezed my hand and said, "Lisa I will see to it that your Mother is rolled in here before you leave for Houston. This is for the best that you go to Houston. I have been talking to the Doctors down there. They will be prepared to give you every special treatment you need. My church will be praying for you. Now I am going to make arrangements for you to see your Mother and to be checked out." Doctor Cagle gently let go of my hand as he stepped away from my bed. The nurses in the room followed his lead as they both smiled at me as though everything was going to be ok. l They assured me that there would be no problem. They would bring her right down to see me.

I think that my reaction to the news alarmed the doctors. They saw that I was not excited about leaving Mother or riding in a helicopter, so they administered more medication in an attempt to keep me as relaxed as possible. Mother was soon rolled into my room in a wheelchair so that she could say goodbye to me. I tried my best to act as though my heart was spilling over with courage for this journey that I was about to embark upon. Despite my effort, Mother could see the fear written all over my face. I did not want to leave Nacogdoches. She spoke words of faith to me and reminded me that our true healing and strength came from our Lord and Savior. I tried to grasp this fact, knowing that I would have the angels and the Lord with me every step of the way. But still, knowing that my father and mother would be miles away from me was very disturbing. I was a homebody kid. I had never really been away from home. A couple of very short church trips were my only times away from them. Besides that, I had always had my Mother or Dad right beside me every step of the way through my short life's adventures. Now I was going into the big city in a helicopter, accompanied by people I had never met before.

Mother was not able to stay with me for very long. She was still so weak that she had to be taken back to her hospital bed. I noticed that tears began to fill her eyes. She had been in her room for a short while when Aunt Bernice, my mother's sister-in-law, called to check on both of our conditions. As soon as Mother realized who they were speaking to on her phone, she asked to speak with Aunt Bernice. She had a request from one mother to another. With a shaky voice, she explained to Aunt Bernice that they were preparing to transport me to Houston. Aunt Bernice assured mother that it was for the best. All my doctors agreed that I needed more intensive care than Nacogdoches could provide. Mother then explained to Aunt Bernice that she needed to ask a special favor from her. She knew that Aunt Bernice had come through for the family many times over the years. She had faith she would come through for her again. "Bernice, will you go to Houston and be with Lisa? I don't want her to be alone down there." Aunt Bernice did not hesitate for even a second as she assured Mother that she would pack her suitcase and be in Houston when I landed. Daddy had to leave the hospital the same day. He wanted to take care of legal matters concerning Devin. He didn't want him to be paroled before the trial date. Daddy also was going to go by the house and check on Ben and Alex. For the first crucial days, Ben and Alex where allowed to stay in the Hill's home. Mrs. Hill even drove them to school so they wouldn't have to face kids on the bus. Daddy soon turned to Candy to return home and look after them while Mother and he were both away. Daddy was in the district attorney's office when he received word that I was going to be sent to Houston. He turned to Lynne, my first cousin on my mother's side, who was standing beside him. Lynn had accompanied Daddy to see the district attorney.

Lynne looked into Daddy's eyes and could see his overwhelming anguish. He quickly asked, "J. L., is there anything I can do to help?"

Daddy took a deep breath and asked, "Lynne, can you go to Houston and be with Lisa until I can make some other arrangements?"

Lynne did not waver. He assured Daddy that he would get right on it, and not to worry. Lynne said, "As soon as I know something about Lisa's condition I will call you. J. L., don't you worry. Lisa is going to make it. And I will be right there with her, every step of the way." Lynne had to do far more than just pack his bags and head to Houston. He owned his own business and had to go home and make arrangements with his wife to help him. His clients had to be notified that he would not be doing anymore jobs for anyone for the time being.

The helicopter summoned to take me to Houston did not arrive in Nacogdoches until late in the evening, but once it finally arrived, the doctors immediately loaded me on board. Rex had volunteered to ride in the helicopter with me to help keep me calm during the flight. Unfortunately, there was no room for Rex on the helicopter. But he managed to tell me a special goodbye as they prepared me. Rex looked into my eyes as though the world around him had stopped and said, "Lisa, I love you and you are going to be alright. You are brave and strong in your faith. I will be praying for you and will be to Houston to see you as soon as possible. Remember I love you."

The flight went by quickly and without incident, just as the doctors had anticipated. My welcoming committee at the hospital seemed to be off-duty when I arrived. Aunt Bernice and Lynne had met up with each other at the hospital. To their dismay, the hospital refused to admit me to their care. I was taken to another hospital and rejected again, despite being insured by one of the best insurance companies in the USA. Finally, I was taken to Texas Children's hospital, where I was admitted.

There, Dr. Matthew Poke decided to take me under his wing. He was a top-notch pediatric surgeon who took a long, hard look at me during his initial examination. He believed that he could lead me down the road to full recovery. I was taken immediately to surgery. There the doctors took a closer look at the massive injuries and formed a game plan. I was then taken into ICU and placed in the back of the room in a corner. I was near the windows facing the front of the hospital. I really didn't remember seeing Aunt Bernice and Lynne that night, but first thing the next morning, they both walked into ICU during visiting hours. They explained they were there to stay with me. I lay in the bed as aware of the circumstances surrounding me as could be expected. My memory of my family and home life was, for the most part, intact.

Dr. Fernando Stein, the pediatric doctor at Texas Children, came out to speak with Lynn and Aunt Bernice to describe what I was facing medically. He explained that the odds were not good and that I was in very serious condition. He assured them that he and his staff would do everything medically possible to bring me through this difficult time in my life.

Lynne told Doctor Stein that I was going to survive no matter what I faced medically, because there were many people back home praying. Doctor Stein did not hesitate, explaining that he would also be praying and trusting the Lord to intervene with his healing hand. Lynne had made a commitment to my Daddy that he would help take care of me. Lynne could not give up on me because as a father, he knew it would destroy something inside Daddy, and no one in the family wanted to see that happen.

Then I saw Lynne, and I was quite surprised that he had chosen to come to my side to help. Drilled in my head was what my mother had always told me about Lynne's immediate family.

Never in my young life had I ever seen my cousin Lynne at family reunions or at gatherings at my grandparents' home. Yet my mother often reflected on the godly life his family had chosen to live. She used them to encourage me during times that I was struggling with being a Christian. I used my hands to motion for something to write with, and I wrote Lynne a note. I told him how much I had always admired him and that I had heard nothing but good things about him. When I had finished writing, Lynne read my note.

"Lisa, thank you. I have always thought highly of Uncle J.L. and Aunt Reba. I know you don't know me that well, but I will be here by your side with Aunt Bernice until they send you home," he said after reading my note. As we looked into each other's eyes, I could see his comment had come from deep within. I was looking forward to getting to know him.

I was not surprised one bit that Aunt Bernice had come to my side to support me. She had a history of being there for people in need. It didn't matter what kind of assistance was called for.

The few weeks I was in Texas Children's Hospital seemed to go by so slowly. For the first two weeks, I was only coherent and aware of my surroundings when the medication brought me out of semi-conscious. The first surgery I had underwent when arriving was more than my weary body could handle, so I was medicated to the point I didn't know who was by my bedside. Lynn had insisted that he or Aunt Bernice be allowed to be by my bed side. The Doctors started medicating me less, allowing me to be more aware of what was taking place. It seemed that every time I was doing better, there was a set back. My fever kept going so high that they had to put an ice pack in the bed, under my whole body. When they would turn it on, I got so cold my teeth would chatter, and I would beg them to turn it off. But my begging was to no avail. They would quietly explain to me, "Not till your fever comes down." Lying naked on the bed with the very cold ice pack, with machines and IVs hooked up to me, my mind began to wonder why all this had happened. It was a hard thing to ponder. I began to let my mind drift into the world I'd known before the day that forever changed my life.

FIRST ATTRACTION

When I entered seventh grade inside it felt like I was walking in high cotton. Besides being allowed to play sports, the next coolest thing for me was a free lunch period. This meant that I could eat wherever I wanted, off campus, cafeteria, gym, agriculture shop, or anyplace else. It had a way of making me feel so independent and on top of the world in its own unique way. My close friends and I chose the agriculture shop where a lot of students from the seventh to twelfth grades hung out.

Devin and I mostly just spoke to each other during the first few weeks of school. Then it became more words and "the stare." "The stare" was something all my friends noticed right away. Next thing I know, everyday at lunch, my classmates were teasing me. I just denied anything was developing acted as though their teasing wasn't bothering me. It was the third week of school when I heard Stephanie say, "Lisa, here he comes. We told you!" I looked up, and sure enough my heart froze as I saw Devin walking straight toward me. My friends all smirked, and I found myself at a loss for words. After a few days of stuttering and awkwardness, we learned how to talk about many things to pass the time. So, from that day, wherever I sat or went to eat, Devin was right there. He would speak kindly, making his presence known. As the days passed at school, I found myself enjoying our brief lunch hour visits. I began to see a side of Devin that I felt no one else ever saw. I found myself beginning to trust his actions and believe in the words he spoke.

Before long, Devin showed me a kind heart through his tender words. They caused me to allow him to see my vulnerable side. My friends soon saw that the attraction Devin had for me was being reciprocated. Soon, our short lunch hour visits grew to seeing one another before school and in-between classes. To all my friends, I was Devin's girl. I kept denying any such relationship. I tried so hard to keep my feelings and emotions locked inside my cold heart.

Basketball was what I'd dreamed of from as far back as I could remember. It all started in a West Sabine gym where I used to watch my sister play ball. I always sat as close to the court as possible, hoping I could talk to some of the teenage players. It didn't take me long to memorize everyone's style of play. Every player had something that stood out to me, something that I would go home and practice doing myself. Each day that I got closer to being a seventh grader, my heart leaped for joy. Finally, that day came, and signing up for basketball was at the top of my list. From the first day of school when we all met Coach Rice and heard his welcoming lecture, I started dreaming. My dreams were accompanied by practicing in the backyard under the security light every night. I would often stay late, no matter how tired I was. I quit only when I heard Mother call for me to come in the house for the night. It didn't take my friends at school long to learn that basketball and my Lord and Savior were all I thought about. Coach Rice even helped lift my expectations higher by allowing me to play a couple of games with the eighth graders.

THE FIRST
SIGN OF DANGER

While lying in that hospital bed when no one was in the room to visit me, all I could think about was Devin. My worst fears of him had come true. However, it felt as though it had been a lifetime since the shooting. My fever finally began coming down. Then they were able to treat me with antibiotics rather than the ice treatment. I had been through several surgeries since I had arrived in Houston. Yet due to my internal injuries, I was still in a critical condition. My family and friends came in to see me on regular visits, but no more than two or three visitors at a time were allowed. The waiting room was never without family members giving their support. Within a few days, two visitors arrived in the waiting room. Their names were Mr. and Mrs. Jefferson. They had first heard my story on the national news. Mrs. Jefferson was so overwhelmed by the story that she went to her beauty shop with it heavy on her heart. There she discovered that the church she attended had personal information. One of my in-laws had relatives that attended the same church. They had been called and asked to pray. Mrs. Jefferson found out from her church that I had been air-lifted to a Houston hospital. Mr. and Mrs. Jefferson came into the waiting room that evening asking if there were any family members for Lisa Barnett present. Lynn and Aunt Bernice answered the concern of the couple who where coming to give their spiritual support. Aunt Bernice brought the couple in to see me and introduced them as a local pastor and his wife. They briefly spoke, but then asked my favorite question, "May we pray for you, Lisa?" I quickly nodded my head with a smile on my face because I had enough sense to know I needed a lot of prayer.

I spent all the time I had with the doctors and nurses asking them one question: Are you born again! It was weighing heavy on my heart that I might not live to see tomorrow. What, then, was the last thing I wanted to do on earth? One thought came to my mind: spread the gospel, lead people to salvation. I was so medicated that it never seemed strange to me that no matter who I asked the question, they all said yes with a smile on their face.

I had been in ICU for about a week when suddenly a thought popped into my mind. Why didn't I see the bad side of Devin until it was too late to do anything? I remembered the one warning sign I had, but it was my nature to give everyone a second chance. Starring out the window by my bed it was late in the afternoon watching people walking on the side walk. It as though I left the hospital bed and went back to a day that was forever sketched in my memory. It was late in the afternoon when Sam, Candy, and Ben rode off on their horses. It was almost sunset when Alex and I heard the horses running rapidly down the dirt road. Candy was in the lead and she began screaming as soon as she saw the James', who were working in their yard.

Candy's words rang out loud and clear: "He pulled a gun on us, that SOB. He pulled a *gun* on us," she said. Candy and Ben then rode up to our house.

Daddy, hearing all the commotion, came around to see what Ben and Candy were upset about. Even Mother came out of the house to learn what had just happened. After hearing the story, Daddy went inside the house to call the police. The James family then came over to our yard. Daddy and Mr. James questioned Ben, Sam, and Candy on all the details about the threat. We all listened intently to the story. A few minutes later a deputy sheriff arrived at our house to take a report. I stood at a distance in the light watching Candy, Ben, Sam, Daddy, and Mr. James, talk to the deputy.

Darkness surrounded us except for the security light. We all sat or stood under its glow as fear gripped my soul. I felt that the whole gun incident was my fault. If I had just not told Ben what Leo and Adam had said to me about Adam's motorcycle tire picking up a piece of glass while Devin seem to orchestrated the whole episode. I had turned to Ben for help because I was scared but all I caused was a gun pulling. I should have known right then and there if Devin would pull a gun on my family and friend that he was dangerous. When I told Ben how I had been threatened on our dirt road, anger rushed through his veins. In his eyes no jerk on a motorcycle was going to threaten anyone in his family. Guilt began to consume my inner being as a thought went through my mind. What if they had gotten killed or shot? I knew Ben wanted to beat the crap out of him, but he didn't have a gun, only a club. But Devin first had a machete, then produced a gun. *Dear God* ,I cried inside, *this isn't fair. Why couldn't Devin just have an old-fashioned fist fight!* The story was told that Devin pulled a machete first. But when Candy showed him the club, he then pulled out the gun!

Daddy and Mr. James followed up with the Sheriff's department about pressing charges against Devin. It was only a few weeks until the court convened again. Strangely enough, Devin was talking to me at school as though he had done nothing wrong. We did not really talk much about the gun incident. Yet when I looked into Devin's eyes, something inside me made me believe that he would have never pulled that trigger. He kept assuring me that it was self-defense, that he had no choice. He was out-numbered, and they had a club.

I was home mowing the yard the day Ben, Candy, and Daddy drove up in the driveway. They had news of the verdict regarding the gun incident. To our shock and dismay, Devin was found innocent on the grounds of self-defense. Alex was the one who came to me and told me the news. The way Alex said it to me pierced my heart like a dagger. He had walked up to me with a cold, harsh look on his face and got right in my face to say, "Your boyfriend won at court." I felt about two inches tall. I was not Devin's girlfriend. We were only acquaintances at school. I had to admit, however, that I had begun to enjoy his company. I now knew, that if my own brother thought I was Devin's girlfriend, probably everyone at school thought the same.

ARE YOU BORN AGAIN

Lying in the ICU with all of that on my mind brought tears to my eyes. My tears of heartache soon went to tears of pain as my condition took over my thoughts, away from any thoughts about Devin. I was getting worse and had only been in Houston for a few weeks. The doctors were having a hard time controlling my internal injuries. I was requiring more blood because of the internal bleeding. The infection kept getting worse instead of better. Late one day I was feeling very weak, when suddenly I began hemorrhaging. Blood started coming out of my trachea. The doctors and nurses ran to my side. I remember feeling like a water fountain as I opened my mouth and blood came out. The nurse on duty ran to the phone to notify my surgeon about my unfortunate turn for the worse. Suddenly, I was being rushed to the pre-operation room while the doctors scrubbed in for another surgery. Lynne and Aunt Bernice, who were in the waiting room, had to make another now-familiar phone call to Daddy in Nacogdoches. Aunt Bernice or Lynne would need to sign the papers and also be a witness. The head nurse called and informed Daddy as to what was happening. Lynne could not bear the thought of my waiting for surgery without him being by my side, to offer me some comfort and an explanation as to what was taking place. So Lynne asked to be allowed to wait with me in spite of the rule of no one being allowed inside the holding room. Doctor Stein agreed, but warned Lynne that I did not look well at all nor did all the blood on my bed. Lynne hastily made his way back to the holding room where I lay. He saw a bed that was covered with blood, so much that it had even spilled onto the floor. It looked as though I were in a war zone. Lynne bit his upper lip as he took my bloody hand and began explaining to me what was happening. Lynne spoke of faith and hope to me, despite the fear that was hidden behind his eyes. All he could think about was the promise he had made to Dad. A promise from one father to another that he would stand in the gap, both physically and spiritually, until Dad could take my hand himself.

There was one thing heavy on my heart that I had to do before I went to surgery. I wrote on my clipboard that I wanted to see the surgical team. I wrote on the board "Are you born again?" and held it up for each of them to read. I slowly reached over and took one of my bloody fingers and pointed to each one of them and then to the question. Each time I touched the clipboard, blood stained the paper.

The surgical team seemed to be bothered by my question to the point that behind closed doors, they asked if another team could be called in because they felt bad about lying to me. Doctor Poke quickly told them there was no one else available, and the surgery could not be put off. They where instructed to pull themselves together and head for the operating room.

This surgery was hard on Aunt Bernice and Lynne as they waited into the night. Lynne knew in his gut that I was probably at one of the worst stages of my recovery. It was probably the worst condition that I had been in since I had survived that first week while fighting to stay alive. After several hours had passed, the doctors finally came out of the swinging doors with somewhat good news. To Aunt Bernice and Lynne, it was a relief that I had made it through the surgery.

That good news concerned what they had decided to do during surgery about my injured esophagus. The doctors explained that they had cut my esophagus in two and took out the most damaged section, which consisted of eighty to ninety percent of it. They explained that now my esophagus would be out the side of my neck where a bag would be attached and changed when needed. Near my stomach, the doctors had stapled off the other end of my esophagus. I would continue to have a g-tube where liquid food would be given to me. They believed this would give my internal injuries a chance to heal, but they would not know for a few days.

It was touch-and-go for the first few days. The pain I felt after waking up from surgery was overwhelming. It felt like every organ on the inside of my body had been beaten with a baseball bat. I realized that I had been to surgery. Once I was completely awake, I was rather confused as to why I had a hole in the side of my neck. I recognized Lynne and Aunt Bernice before I saw my two main doctors. After seeing that I was finally awake, Lynne started to explain what had happened. Lynne always had a way of making me understand what was happening.

I was most relieved to discover that I was not tied to the bed as I had been the first week in ICU, like a caged animal. When Doctor Todd had implanted a trachea, he felt I needed to be tied to the bed, otherwise I might accidentally pull it out and do damage that could not be repaired. Thanks to Lynne, I did not have to lie there, miserable and unaware of what was going on for very long. The moment Lynne came into the room, he untied me, despite the nurse telling him not to. Lynne explained to her that I needed to understand what was in my neck and what was happening. Sure enough, before he left the room that night, I understood what had happened. Best of all, I quit fighting to try to get the straps loose from my arms. Now, once again, Lynne was able to explain to my satisfaction why the doctors had rerouted my esophagus out the side of my neck.

A few days passed slowly, and I began a turn for the better. I was making some improvement, which put smiles on everyone's faces. The nurses began sitting me higher up in the bed. This allowed me to see almost all the way down the ICU room. Something right across from me caught my attention, and I began to laugh. There was a baby in a crib. His parents had bought the baby a monkey puppet. They were using it to talk to the baby as he lay there with his eyes wide open. This scene was amazing to me. Aunt Bernice had come in to visit with me and saw that the monkey had my full attention. More important even, the parents of the baby also realized I was watching and laughing for the first time in many weeks.

Those parents spoke to each other in what I thought was Spanish. Then the father, with the monkey in his hand, walked over to Aunt Bernice and pointed to me. She was not sure what the gentleman was trying to say, so she turned to a nurse who knew how to speak their language. The nurse talked to the gentleman. Then, with a smile on her face, she explained that they wanted me to have the monkey as a gift.

Aunt Bernice took the monkey, walked over to me and handing the monkey to me, said, "They noticed how much you were enjoying watching it from over here." I was astonished that these people who we did not know were being so kind. I had to choke back my tears. On an impulse, I picked up a pink teddy bear that was very special to me. I handed it to Aunt Bernice and pointed to the baby. Aunt Bernice said, "Lisa, do you want to give this teddy bear to the baby?" I quickly nodded my head yes. Aunt Bernice walked over to present my gift.

This pink teddy bear had been in the bed with me ever since my classmates had come to see me in Houston. That was a special visit I had with them, because I was able to communicate with them. I could write on a clipboard and was able to remember their visit. It was unlike the visits at Nacogdoches where, most of the time, they saw me only from a distance, and usually I was unconscious from medication. Lying in the bed with my monkey, I began to think about kindness. In a strange way, it made me think about Devin. Suddenly, my mind was a million miles away, back in a time that seemed so innocent.

THE DANCE

Valentine's Day was approaching and most of my girlfriends were giddy with expectation. As for me, it was just going to be another day at school, a day I had anticipated when I would be teasing and joking around with everyone about their beaus. Little did I know I was in for a big surprise. During lunchtime Devin and I talked while everyone else was playing "goggle eyes" over their Valentine presents.

Lunch time was almost over. Devin and I were standing in the Jr. High hallway when he excused himself, saying he needed to go do something, but would be right back. I used that time to get my books out of the locker and visit with some friends. It was only a moment before Devin returned holding a big sack in his hand. We met back at our usual spot in the hallway. Devin, with a smile on his face said, "I got you something for Valentine's Day. I hope you like it." He gently handed the bag to me, "Open it," he urged.

My heart seemed to skip beats because up to this point, Devin had only been a friend. What was I going to tell my friends? How could I act like we were only friends, when this indicated we were far more! A part of me was speechless, while the other part was screaming on the inside, "Run, run!" I pulled out a large, heart shaped box of chocolate candy with a card attached. Still not saying anything, I opened the card, only to be more shocked. The card said in big letters on the front, "TO MY WIFE." When I saw the words, I could not bring myself to look at Devin again. My emotions raced. My feelings were shallow compared to how deep and serious Devin's feelings apparently were. Without looking at Devin, and out of pure politeness I said, "Thank you, I like it." Devin seemed to begin expressing a serious statement, when the bell interrupted his sentence.

I used the bell as my escape out of a sensitive situation. I couldn't get into the classroom quick enough. I was wishing that I could just disappear into thin air. Instead, all my friends circled my desk asking "What did Devin get you?" I tried to ignore them. I was torn between looking at them and at Devin, who I could see out the window walking to his class in the science building. My friends persisted until I showed them the box of candy, but I refused to show them the card. I tried to block those words from my mind.

The candy box was so big it wouldn't fit in my locker along with all my text books. For that reason, I had to carry it from class to class for the rest of the day. The attention it got only made me more nervous about what my family would say when I got home with it.

The final bell came soon enough for me that day. The bus ride went by way too quickly. When I got off the bus at my stop, I walked as slowly as possible up to the house. Alex didn't give me a chance to explain to anyone. He shouted out the news of my Valentine's Day gift as soon as he opened the front door.

After stepping inside, I heard Candy come out of her room saying, "You've got to be joking!" I suppose the guilty look on my face said it all, as I kept the candy box partially hidden behind my back.

Mother was sitting on the couch. She began to laugh and then explained why. Candy had never been given a box of candy for Valentine's Day. Mother continued to tease Candy, and in a way relieved my stress.

Candy came up to me and said, "Let me see what he bought." When I showed her the box, she was surprised to see that it was the largest one that our hometown store sold. She teased me, "Here, let me show you the secret to eating chocolate candy." She walked over to the fireplace and said, "Give me the candy and go in the kitchen and bring back a knife and a saucer." I grudgingly did as she instructed, wondering what she was up to. When I returned, I saw that Candy had opened the candy and had one large piece in her hand. She explained, as I sat beside her, that we were to cut each one open. If we liked what was inside, we ate it. But if we didn't, we put it back in the box and left it for someone else, like Mother for instance, to eat. Mother scolded Candy because that was a bad habit she was teaching me, and she should to be ashamed of herself. Candy and I continued on with our game until we had found all the good pieces, ignoring Mother's complaint.

This recollection didn't make my heart shatter into pieces nearly as badly as my next memory. Seventh grade was a big step for my class, especially when it came to older boyfriends and birthday parties. No longer were birthday parties just cake, ice-cream, and pin-the-tail-on-the-donkey. Instead, they were dancing parties, and most of all, parties where you were asked out on a date! Without warning, Devin and I began running into each other at these parties. My friends always said that he only came looking for me. I was at Jane Carlson's thirteenth birthday party when I finally realized just how interested Devin was in building our relationship.

When Devin entered the room that night, it was as though our eyes locked on each other. I almost fell out of my chair when Devin asked me for a dance. After using every excuse I could think of, I finally said, "Only if it is okay with Ben." Immediately Devin walked right over and asked Ben for permission to dance with me. Ben, in a mischievous moment said yes, knowing that I was counting on him to say no. He also had an ulterior motive— with me dancing with Devin, I would be too busy to keep messing up his make-out sessions with Jane Carlson, the birthday girl and one of my real good friends.

Ben and Sam were both dating two of my classmates, Jane Carlson and Carla Moody respectively. That night when Devin walked in and there wasn't a fight, I was very thankful. I felt as though Ben saying I could dance with Devin was like a sign of peace between the two of them since the gun-pulling and court date.

Devin returned and grasped my hand and escorted me to the dance floor. My heart seemed to melt. I could feel everyone's eyes staring at us. I knew this would be all over town before sunrise. Now I was openly showing that I had an interest in Devin that was far past a friendship. Devin and I danced that night as though no one else was in the room. He held me very gently, not too close, but close enough that I could hear his heart beating. We didn't talk much. Instead, we just enjoyed the moment, hoping it would last forever. However, all too soon, the party came to a close.

Devin left first, but not before letting everyone in the room know that he had been there strictly to see me. It was this night that I had looked into Devin's eyes and slowly began to trust and believe in him.

This was what made the shooting such a heartache; a heartache that would never go away. Devin was someone in whom I trusted and felt would never do me harm.

Devin began making his appearances with me more obvious, especially at school. He started opening up to me about how he desired to be thought of as more than just a friend or acquaintance. At this point, a friend was all that I would admit that we were to each other. Soon it seemed that our relationship had drifted into a more serious stage. Devin now expressed to me how serious he was about his desire to go far beyond just being a close friend. I still remember the look in his eyes the day he asked if he could take me out on a date. My first response was not the most courteous I ever gave anyone. I laughed and said, "You've got to be joking."

Not taking no for an answer, he responded, "No, I'm not joking. I will have you home by your curfew, I promise." I explained to him that my father would not even consider my dating until I was sixteen. Even then, it would have to be with someone he approved of. Devin let his idea of our dating drop, but certainly not how he felt about me.

Devin told me that seeing each other at school wasn't enough. He wanted to see me more often. He even told me that he cared for me very deeply. The more he talked about these things, the more nervous I became. My feelings were far from being as serious as Devin's were for me, but I did have an interest in Devin that I found rather intriguing. I often would look at Devin intently as he talked, and wondered if I could ever really love this cowboy. My heart indeed cared for Devin enough that I feared hurting his feelings or letting him down in some way. I had always been a sensitive and caring person. There was a special place in my thirteen-year-old heart that I had reserved for a very special boy. I was only in seventh grade, but I could tell how boys looked at us younger girls. As each day passed, I began to feel my heart melting and myself allowing it to open up more and more for Devin.

It was only a couple of days later that Devin came to school with a whole new plan. He'd thought of a way to see me more often. He had asked his mother if she would chaperone us at their house while we watched a movie and ate popcorn. We would be supervised and not left alone. Therefore, my parents could relax and be willing to let me go. I explained to Devin that to my parents, it would still be a date. If he thought this idea would fly, he would have to ask my parents' permission for me to go to his house. Of course, he wasn't deterred. He assured me that he had no problem asking my parents because he was so confident they would say yes.

Sure enough, a few days later, Devin called our house desiring to speak with Mother. He explained his brainstorm and asked for Mother's approval for that weekend. Mother firmly said no. The conversation didn't go much further. Devin was rather surprised. He was more upset than anything with such a definite no. It still remained no, even after he'd talked with Mother a second time.

That week at school, Devin and I discussed what Mother's refusal meant for the two of us. For me it just meant that we would have to wait until I was older. For Devin, it meant he had to come up with another plan. I could see that look in his eyes, the look that told me he wasn't going to give up on the notion of us seeing one another more often. That look in his eyes was a mere glimpse of what I would see in the future. Devin's eyes were filled with a passion for me that seemed to overwhelm his every thought. There was an angry fire deep in the center of his soul that challenged this obstacle. How dare someone try to keep us apart!

THE SPECIAL VISITS IN ICU

I finally realized that I had to put these thoughts out of my mind and try to focus on what was at hand. This meant working toward my recovery. A weekend had passed, and many of my family members had come to see me in the hospital. I made a discovery that caused everyone to laugh. After visiting hours, my stomach began hurting, so I signaled for the nurse. She summoned the doctor on duty to examine my concern. The doctor, one that had never tended to me, came over and uncovered me. The sheet was just covering my hips and up to my waist. I realized I had on no underwear on. This made me feel very uncomfortable. The doctor finished his exam, wrote in my chart, and left my bed side.

The nurse covered my bottom back up. She saw I was not a happy camper. I wrote on my clipboard when I could to see my Aunt Bernice again. She assured me that I'd be seeing her very soon.

Before Aunt Bernice arrived, my pediatrician, Dr. Stein, arrived to make his rounds. I had built a kinship with Dr. Stein. I felt free to express my discontent to him. I wrote on the clipboard that I wanted my underwear back on. A big smile came across his face. He responded that he would see to that right away. After leaving my bedside, Dr. Stein walked into the waiting room. My family was waiting for visiting hours. Dr. Stein reported my request to my family. He knew for a fact that I had made some significant improvement, as I had asked for some underwear. This meant I was now well aware of my surroundings and understood more of what was going on concerning my care. My family laughed at this. My first cousin on my mother's side, Sylvia, immediately responded, "I am going to buy Lisa some underwear right now."

During my next visiting hour, I was granted my wish and given underwear to put on. This made me feel more decent, under the circumstances. I received more news that blessed my soul from deep within the walls of that hospital. The towns of Hemphill and Pineland had pulled together to have a fundraiser day on the county square for our family. Bills had been mounting at the house from day one, but now our family, life-long friends, and loved ones were pulling together to help us through a difficult time. An account was set up at the bank for people to make a love offering on our behalf.

It wasn't long after this weekend that plans were made to move me out of ICU. One thing was really bearing on my mind. I was asking Aunt Bernice, "When am I going to get to see my Maw Maw?" Unfortunately, Maw Maw, my grandmother, had died the past October. But in my bewildered mind, she was still alive. I had not accepted her death whatsoever. I apparently had blocked out of my mind that whole week when we had all said goodbye to Maw Maw.

Aunt Bernice talked to the doctors about my request. They instructed her not to remind me that Maw Maw had died. Rather, they should let me remember it in my own time. Aunt Bernice had received special permission from the doctors to have a TV and VCR brought into the ICU. Then she could play videos of my family, especially Maw Maw. The doctors readily agreed to this. They felt it would be good therapy for me to watch videos of my past healthy experiences with my family.

I lay in the bed that day looking forward to watching the video as Aunt Bernice got everything ready. The play button was finally started, and what a smile it put on my face. I watched my family gathering at Uncle Knox's home to celebrate Maw Maw's birthday.

Watching my aunts and uncles cut up with each other did not trigger anything in my memory, except for one close-up of Maw Maw, and when I heard her voice, I remembered that she was gone. Tears welled up in my eyes. I looked at my Aunt Bernice and wrote on my clipboard, "That was her last birthday party before she died, wasn't it?" Aunt Bernice, seeing me cry, confirmed it. My Maw Maw *couldn't* come to see me. She was dead and in a better place now. A short time later, Aunt Bernice had to leave because visiting hours were over. I tried so hard not to think about how much I missed Maw Maw. But Aunt Bernice *did* give me something to look forward to. She told me that Mother and Dad were coming to see me in just a few days.

Mother had been released from the Nacogdoches hospital. Unfortunately the rebuilding of her arm had not even begun. Dr. Jorgensen had placed a bar sticking outside Mother's arm to hold it together while her arm was in a splint. It spanned from right below her elbow to her wrist. They were giving the gunshot wound ample time to heal. Dr. Jorgensen wanted Mother to see a very highly-recommended doctor in Houston. He had attempted to make an appointment with him for Mother, but had been unsuccessful. Daddy and Aunt Bernice felt the trip to Houston was still something Mother needed to do so she could see me in person.

Aunt Bernice had a nephew who owned an airplane. He offered to fly Mother to Houston to avoid the long car ride. Several days passed, and finally the day arrived. Mother and Dad were on their way to Houston. They were picked up at the airport and brought straight on to the hospital. I had been elevated as high as my hospital bed would go. I was looking down the ICU ward waiting for Mother to appear. I could not really remember seeing Mother in Nacogdoches, so seeing her now would feel like it was the first time since our separation at the scene of the shooting.

I was wide awake when I heard the doors to the ICU being opened. I knew this meant visiting hours were beginning. I saw people I didn't know walking down the hall. Then, at a distance, I spied Mother walking beside Aunt Bernice. A huge smile came to my face. When we made eye contact, I opened my mouth as though I could speak. I attempted to mouth a word that I knew Mother wished so much to hear audibly.

Aunt Bernice spoke first, "I know what Lisa was trying to say. She was saying "Mother." When they reached my bedside, Aunt Bernice found a chair for Mother to sit in. The trip had made Mother very weak. I found my paper and clipboard and started writing to Mother exactly what was on my mind. The main thing I wanted to tell her was something I had not shared with anyone—seeing the warrior angels in the sky immediately after we were shot.

I revealed to Mother by writing on a clip board that when I collapsed and fell to the ground, I looked into the sky, and the first thing I saw were two warrior angels descending from heaven. This encouraged and assured me in an awe-inspiring way that my heavenly Father was going to help me fight my battle. We would be victorious in the end. After I had shared with her what I had seen, she reaffirmed the thought. Mother took my hand and looked deep into my eyes. She told me that the Lord was not just on the throne, but beside me every step of the way. I was going to be okay. I could tell by looking at Mother that she was fighting tears of joy. God had become more real and personal to me. Mother took a deep breath as she looked up at Aunt Bernice and said, "The angels are here with you, although you can not see them. They are going to guard you and minister to you. All you have to do is have faith in the God we serve that we are all going to make it through this valley." Due to Mother's weakness from the trip, she could not stay at my bedside long before having to depart.

Arrangements had been made for Mother and Dad to stay in a nearby motel. However, those plans soon changed when Dr. Stein was notified that Mother had come down for a visit. He arranged for Mother to be admitted to Memorial Hospital, which was located next to Texas Children's Hospital. He also arranged for the best-known bone doctor in Houston to examine Mother.

Mother stayed one night at Memorial and was evaluated by Dr. Bennett. He explained to the family that unless a limb had two strong blood vessels working, the limb could not be saved. Mother still only had one blood vessel that was operating. We were all standing on faith alone that Mother's arm would be saved. She was given the opportunity to remain in Houston and change doctors. Perhaps she should get yet another opinion about saving her arm. Despite Doctor's opinion, Mother's inner spirit told her to return to Nacogdoches and allow her doctor to finish what he had started. She also had to have faith in her heavenly Father that she was going to be okay. She had to trust in God that I could make it without her by my side.

Mother made three or four trips to the ICU to see me for short visits. Now it was time to say goodbye. Mother and Daddy were about to leave when my doctors informed my family that I needed another surgery. I would be going down that long hallway to the operating room once again. At the same time, Mother would be leaving the hospital for home. The doctors explained everything to me, but I am not sure that I understood everything they were saying. Instead what sank deep into my heart was that Mother was leaving, and I wanted so badly to get up out of the bed and go home with Mother and Dad, as good as new.

Candy, Alex, and a friend, Candy Rueffer, drove down in a van to give Mother and Dad a ride home. When I heard that Alex was in the waiting room, I signaled my nurse. I realized that it wasn't visiting hours, and he was too young, but I wanted to see him so badly. I scribbled my request on my clipboard for the nurse. To my delight, the request was granted. The nurse elevated my bed so that I could see down the ICU walkway. I saw the nurse and Alex coming through the ICU room toward my bed. The nurse had her hand on Alex's shoulder as they slowly walked up to my bed. I just wanted to tell Alex that I loved him and would be home soon. I wrote on my clipboard, and the nurse showed Alex what I had written. Alex stood there speechless. There stood my little brother, who seemingly had grown up overnight. I admired his cotton-top head and freckled face. Alex was struggling just to nod his head and tell me he was praying for me. Then the nurse told me it was time for Alex to leave. The nurse escorted Alex out of the ICU. I wanted so badly to jump out of bed and be normal again. I wanted to run and play with Alex again and not lie helplessly like a baby. I worried who was going to help Alex make it through all this. Inside I had a sense of peace knowing that Candy was on the other side of those doors.

Soon afterwards, I was rolled into the waiting room and was on my way to surgery. Now I had to say goodbye to Mother and Dad. Candy also said goodbye to me. While Mother and Dad's faces had worn their carefully prepared, masked expressions, Candy didn't seem to have it all together. I could tell by the look on her face that it was killing her on the inside to see me like this. She was wishing so much that she could take my pain, but it wasn't just my pain she felt as she put her arms around Alex. She reminded him that she was there for him and understood what he was feeling inside. I strained to hold back the tears. I held to my faith, assuring myself that this was just another easy surgery, and I was going to be okay. I knew, for the sake of my family, that I had to put up a brave front. I just smiled and nodded my head as the intern rolled my bed down the long hallway. I felt an amazing peace within, even though my Mother was leaving me and going back home. It was as though the Holy Spirit had gently placed a sense of serenity and peace inside my troubled mind. My life had changed tremendously since the shooting, but I had faith that I was going to be fine.

By the time I came out of surgery, Mother was well on her way home. I was taking a turn for the better. Time began to fly by while in the ICU. There were only a few more visitors which made a lasting impression on my mind.

Caroline and Rex made a trip to see me. Caroline wanted to leave a message with me. She held my hand as she expressed her faith that God was going to heal all of my wounds. I had nothing to fear.

Carl, Ben, and Carl's best friend, Cotter, brought cheer and hope in their own special way. Carl wanted to remind me of how strong I was. I had never let anything knock me down before. He was confident that I would come out victorious. Ben didn't say much, he just told me to hurry up and get well and come back home. Seeing Ben meant a lot to me, because then I was able to see with my own eyes that he was not injured during the shooting. Cotter had his same old funny look about him, saying few words, but with a smile the size of a half-moon.

Candy made a special trip to see me while I was still in the ICU. She brought me news that delighted me in my fragile condition. Candy had a picture for me to see. It was a picture of my brand new niece, Lisa Angelica Barnett. Ron and his wife Scarlet were expecting a baby at the time I was shot. The picture was of Nelly holding her baby sister. *She had been named after me!* That was just the *most special thing* anyone had ever done for me at that time in my life. Lisa Angelica was born January 23, 1986, in Mineola, Texas.

I now had a beautiful reason to fight harder than ever for my life. I wanted to watch Angelica grow up and bloom into a lovely young lady. I wanted to be a worthwhile aunt to her. I knew that this good news would help bring some sunshine back into everyone's lives. Mother and Dad already had two grandsons and two granddaughters. Caroline and Rex had three children, Lee (eleven), Brittany (ten), and Luke (four). Ron and Scarlet had one daughter already, Nelly (five), and now Angelica. Of all seven of Mother and Dad's children, Caroline and Ron were the only ones that were married. This news that I received in ICU made me want to strive harder to be an aunt that all my nieces and nephews could respect and love to be around.

Hemphill School also sent a special message expressing all their thoughts and prayers for me. Coach Franssen came to see me and brought a special gift for me. Coach Gilbert had used a tape player and recorded all my classmates' voices speaking well wishes to me. I was not able to listen to it until Uncle Luke provided a tape player with head phones. Now I knew that the school back home was pulling for me in more ways than I had imagined.

While in ICU, I received a letter from one of my most favorite teachers, Coach Rice. He had written a letter of inspiration, faith, and hope. Aunt Bernice read the letter to me, and it gave me such confidence. It was as though I was playing in the middle of a basketball game and was losing by twenty points. Coach Rice, knowing my family all his life, knew how to make me kick and jump at his command. Aunt Bernice choked up as she read: "Lisa I know you are a fighter and have what it takes to overcome obstacles in life. I have not given up on you because I know you will return to the basketball court. The Lord is going to be with you during this difficult time and remember you are in my prayers." After hearing that letter, I made up my mind then and there, if for no one else but Coach Rice, I would return to the basketball court and make at least two points just for old time's sake.

One of my last days in ICU, Uncle Cullen's pastor, Brother Digmon, came to see me and pray for me. As I looked into his eyes I could see a man that was willing to pay the price when it came to serving God. My parents had known Brother Digmon's family for a number of years before I was even born. When he bowed his head to pray, I could feel the love of God. I closed my eyes at that moment, thankful for the prayer, but knew that I would only rise above the attack of the enemy by the power of God. I didn't know Brother Digmon that well, only that Uncle Cullen always spoke highly of him. I had fond memories of camping and fishing at the lake with Uncle Cullen. His daughter Belinda was a cousin that I could count on. I always loved talking to her because I knew I could confide in her with what was ever on my heart. She was closer to Candy's age, but she always took time to play and visit with Ben, Alex, and me.

I now was truly better. My fever had diminished, and my internal injuries had begun to heal. I had now been in the ICU in Texas Children's for approximately four weeks. I would soon be ready to be moved to a private room, which was very exciting to me. Then I would be able to walk, which would feel great. A physical therapist had been working with me in the ICU. Her methods made absolutely no sense to me. She would lift my legs in the air. Then she would move them as though I was walking on air, although I was not able to assist her. Instead, she would tell me to relax while she worked my muscles for me. This routine made me more eager to prove that I could still walk without assistance.

At long last, Aunt Bernice and Lynne gave me the great news. The doctors were going to move me into a private room. It seemed to take all day to get discharged from ICU. Finally, I was taken out and was on my way to the fourth floor. The room they put me in was small, but at least it had a window that looked out over the front of the hospital. My joy, however, was short lived. Even though I now had a private room, it seemed they increased my treatments. I was put on a schedule of having my back and the side of my lungs patted. The chest therapy was not something that I welcomed, but rather endured. Then I was given breathing treatments so frequently that I felt like I was living on smoke. My physical therapist wasted no time going from bed exercise to putting my feet on the floor. When I stood for the first time, it felt as though all the blood in my head and body rushed to my feet. I became very dizzy. I only took a few feeble steps and was then returned to the bed to rest. I was told not to worry because the dizziness was normal. I was assured that in a few days I would be walking up and down the halls. Sure enough, that was exactly what happened. It was a great feeling the first time I walked down the hallway. That walk turned into a real workout for my weak muscles.

The x-rays of my insides seemed endless. I felt like I had a reserved motel room downstairs in the x-ray department. The x-ray technicians began to tease me, "Lisa, you're back again." They would always do their best to help me laugh about something. They knew that it was not pleasant lying on that cold metal table time and time again.

The day finally came where Doctor Mills walked into the room with a big smile on his face. Doctor Mills said, "This is the day we have been waiting for to see if all the surgeries on your vocal cords where successful." He sat on the edge of my bed and told me how he was going to put a plug in my trachea, which would make it able for me to talk. Lynn and Aunt Bernice quickly had looks of hope and encouragement written all over their faces. Doctor Mills placed the plug in and then asked me to test my vocal cords by speaking. I wasn't sure what to say, so my first words were, "What do you want me to say?" My words were horse, deep, and crackly to say the least. Everyone in the room cheered for me. They all began asking me questions just to get me to speak, but I had a question: why was my voice so different now? Doctor Mills explained that the bullets had paralyzed my left vocal cord, but they where able to repair the right one. He explained how things would be different now, as I wouldn't be able to howl or speak when nervous or at a high tempo. He also explained that until my vocal cords where strong, I would be limited to how much talking I could do in one day. I would have to rest my vocal cords until they were finished healing.

The news I had been wishing for finally found its way into my hospital room in Houston. My doctors were talking about releasing me to continue my recovery at home. I was so excited that I wasn't even worried about my long-term prognosis. The only thing that mattered to me at this point was that I would be leaving the city and heading back to the country. Aunt Bernice and Lynne came into my room one day after having their personal visit with the doctors. They wanted to talk to me. The look on Aunt Bernice's face made me fear bad news. Maybe I might not get to go home after all. They both sat on the bed and took deep breaths before they began speaking.

Lynne began by reminding me that Mother was not in the best condition and had to have a lot of personal attention herself. Aunt Bernice agreed with Lynne, and added that all of this was a lot for my father to handle. Lynne then dove into deeper water and said, "Lisa, you are going to be able to go back home, just not exactly like you thought. The doctors have agreed to let you go home, but you need to stay with me for a while until things are better. Then you can go home with your mother and dad."

I took a long deep breath trying to digest all this, but I realized anything at the moment sounded better than staying in the hospital. Lynne looked deep into my eyes and asked, "Lisa, would you like to go home and stay with me for a while?"

I smiled and promptly said yes. Mother had always spoken highly of Lynne's family.

Lynne continued to explain that he would be leaving soon to go home to make arrangements for me. He would return in a few days to take me home. While he was gone, Aunt Bernice would stay at the hospital with me.

I then asked Aunt Bernice, "Are you coming with me to Lynne's house?" She smiled and said, "Yes, as much stuff as they are sending home with you, we will need two cars to transport everything."

I lay back on my bed while Aunt Bernice and Lynne were talking. I was thinking about what a good a team we were making. We were a trio, and I felt rather special. Lynne left that evening to go back home. I eagerly started getting ready to leave the hospital. The doctors had explained much to Aunt Bernice that I could not hear. But, for the first time, it didn't worry me. When the doctors were not with me, Aunt Bernice helped me walk around the hospital so that I could tell the staff goodbye. The nurses, interns, x-ray technicians, and aides were all happy for me.

Lynne soon returned with his wife Dixie by his side to check me out of the hospital. They spent the first night in a nearby hotel. When the sun rose the next morning, Lynne was at the hospital ready to get everything underway. The staff brought box after box to my room. Each was filled with medical supplies. The boxes also contained Iscal, which was the liquid food they had been feeding me since I became stable in ICU. Around the clock I had either nurses pouring it into me or a machine pumping it in one drop at a time. These had to be loaded in the cars. The day was passing slowly for me, but for Lynne it was going rather fast. They kept taking him out of the room to show him a machine or how to administer certain medications. At last, the day I was longing for was coming to a close.

Early the next morning, waiting to leave the hospital, Aunt Mozelle paid me a visit not knowing I was leaving that day. Aunt Mozelle always had a way of getting everyone's attention in the room by her confident flow of speech. Aunt Mozelle had bought me a musical teddy bear which made me laugh as it played music. Lynne only wanted to speak to the doctors concerning last minute questions, but Aunt Mozelle made sure to her share her joy for my being alive with every doctor that came in the room. Aunt Mozelle was indeed a special aunt to me. We had spent a lot of time sitting in front of a grocery store in Hemphill selling jewelry. Watching Aunt Mozelle in the hospital room made me remember her very words to me as a young child. She had said, "Lisa you have to dress for success and always believing in what you are selling to the customer. Get up early, never sleep late, and from the moment your feet hit the floor, start preparing for a great day." This was a special day for me; I was going home, and I was once again reminded I was loved by many. Aunt Mozelle with her walk and smile that would make Hollywood take notice, with her youngest daughter Angela, who always quietly stood by, said their goodbyes. I watched them depart as I leaned back in my bed and played with my new teddy bear.

I was ready and waiting to leave when something unexpected happened. While sitting on the edge of my bed, fully dressed, I felt liquid running down my pants. I looked down to see that my g-tube had burst and come out of my stomach. All the Isocal they had fed me gushed out. I quickly lay down on the bed and got Aunt Bernice's attention. She notified the nurse who came in to clean me up. Lynne and Dr. Poke came into the room. Dr. Poke looked at Lynne and asked, "Are you ready to go to work?" Lynne, not sure what he meant, gave us a nervous smile. Dr. Poke explained that this event was quite common. It would be something that we would have to deal with at home. He was glad it happened so he could show Lynne exactly what to do when it did.

All of this hit me like a ton of bricks. Dr. Poke calmly stepped over to the bed with a new g-tube in his hand. He told Lynne to get on the other side of the bed and watch what he did. Then he inserted the g-tube into my stomach and pulled it back out. He told Lynne it was now his turn. At that moment, I protested by putting my hand over my stomach and asking, "Do what?" Lynne and Dr. Poke explained how I had to trust Lynne. I had to let him do this or I would have to stay in the hospital because this would recur. I finally agreed, as I kept reminding myself of what Lynne had said. He would take care of me.

Now the moment had come when I had to not only trust Lynne, but I had to let him do his first medical procedure on me. I inhaled quickly and looked over at Aunt Bernice. I was hoping her eyes would reflect assurance and confidence, but it was obvious from the look on Aunt Bernice's face that Lynne was undertaking a task that she would not be able to conduct. I looked down at my stomach to watch. Lynne listened carefully to the doctor's instructions as he inserted the g-tube. Lynne accomplished the task with no problem, and he didn't even seem to break a sweat. Then a big smile came across his face. Lynne gave me the look I had seen many times over the last few weeks. It always encouraged me to know that he had everything under control. He was never a man that ran short on confidence.

That was my first day of wondering just how many similarities my cousin had to our Pa paw, who all the other grandkids called Big Daddy. But my daydreaming was soon ended. We started wrapping up the last few things we needed to do before leaving the hospital. Before long, I found myself walking out the door, down the hallway, and to the elevators. I told all the nurses on my floor goodbye. When we reached the bottom floor, Lynne said, "How would you like to go to the ICU and tell those nurses good-bye? Remember, the last time these nurses had seen you, it was impossible for you to walk or even talk."

Lynne knew that it would mean a lot to them seeing me doing so well. I agreed, and Lynne led the way toward the ICU.

Aunt Bernice, Lynne, Dixie, and I walked through the doors, and soon a crowd of nurses were around me. We shared many smiles and laughs as I told them I was leaving the hospital. Dixie had a camera and started taking pictures for me to keep as we continued to talk about my remarkable improvements.

Suddenly, I felt a lump in my throat, knowing that I needed to express my gratitude. I fought to hold back tears, as I said, "I will never forget what you all did for me, and I thank you from the bottom of my heart. You all did more than just your jobs. You gave me hope during some hard times. Thank ya'll for your help and prayers!" The nurses responded by hugging me and patting me on the back. We walked down stairs to the front door. At last we were on our way home, leaving Houston and heading back to the land I knew and loved.

HOME AWAY
FROM HOME

I assumed that I would be riding with Aunt Bernice, but as I headed toward her car, I was told that I would be riding with Lynne and Dixie. Lynne took me by the arm, led me over to his car, and opened the door. He showed me how he had rearranged the back seat so that I could lie down and rest on the way home. Very soon, we were loaded up and headed out. We were leaving the hospital late in the morning, and this meant we were going to encounter very heavy traffic.

I sat up in the back seat enjoying the scenery as Lynne worked his way to Highway 59. We found traffic at a standstill. By this time, my strength had left me. I had to lay down on the blanket and pillow in the back seat. I told Lynne that if I fell asleep to please wake me up when we could see pine trees again. I fell asleep, and suddenly, Lynne was calling my name. We were nearing his home in Fairmount, Texas. I quickly sat up, eager to look out the window. Although it was a cloudy day, it was a beautiful sight looking across to the forest filled with pine trees. After arriving home late that evening, Lynne's first order of business was getting me to the couch and starting my first feeding expedition. This included hooking up the machines and starting the medical procedures that he had learned at the hospital. Lynne's next order of business was calling Dad. He wanted to let him know that we had made a safe trip and would see him in the morning.

Aunt Bernice spent the first few nights with me at Lynne's house to help me adjust to some changes. The first thing was the tub bath. Aunt Bernice had to help me with this because of all the tubes coming from me and my lack of strength.

Daddy made sure he saw me right away. He came the first morning I was at Lynne's. He wanted to show his faith that everything was going to be alright. When Aunt Bernice told me she had to leave, I felt like a balloon that had just been popped. I had gotten comfortable with Aunt Bernice, Lynne, and me being a team. How could she leave? I was far from being back on my feet. But she promised me that Dixie would take over where she left off. I was not to worry for she would be coming back for frequent visits.

I did my best to hold back tears, because the uncertainties of the future began to hit the walls around my heart like a sledge hammer. I had known Aunt Bernice all my life. I always knew what she was going to say even before the words came out of her mouth. Her actions were etched in stone. This gave me the confidence to lean on her during the storms of life. On the other hand, Lynne was someone I was just getting to know. The last thing I wanted to do was disappoint him in any way. Now here I was, attached at the hip to both Lynne and Dixie. Without their help, I would be up the creek without a paddle.

After a few days passed, I was told that I would be allowed to pay a visit to my home. There, a lot of my family would be gathered. Dixie and Lynne did their usual activities that morning. They came into my bedroom bright and early, ready to start my breathing treatments. They had to connect me to the feeding machine. I wanted to hurry all these procedures along because all I could think about was seeing my house again. I wondered if everything would look the same as I remembered. Perhaps some things had changed since I had been gone. Lynne and Dixie could tell I was very anxious. So, to try and relax me, they began singing southern gospel songs. It truly did take my mind off of going home. Oh, how beautiful and sweet the songs echoed in my ears. Lynne told me stories about how his immediate family used to sing songs in the East Mayfield Baptist Church. I eagerly listened to the family stories. I loved family history. Finally, it was time for me to get dressed for my exciting day. Lynne excused himself while Dixie helped me with my clothes. My heart beat faster at the thought of going home.

We finally left Lynne's house after what seemed like forever. I had prepared myself for the excitement of seeing my home again. But one thing I had not prepared myself for mentally was driving past that church. This was the landmark where it all happened. It was the place that my life had flashed before my eyes as I lay on the ground, blood gushing out of my body. When Lynne rounded the curve, I then saw that church, and it all began to play back to me seemingly in slow motion. It seemed as though I was watching a scary movie. But, no matter how hard I tried, I couldn't seem to turn off the screen. Just as I felt that I was about to scream, Lynne reached back and took my hand. Looking into my eyes, Lynne said, "Lisa, it's okay." The look on Lynne's face gave me a sense of security and confidence that I was okay. It reminded me that I did know the ending to the movie: I lived! Once we were past the church, my thoughts of blood and gunshots slowly faded. I tried to focus again on my excitement of going home for a visit.

When my house finally came into view, unspeakable Joy bubbled out of me. The first person I saw was Daddy. He was on the front porch waiting to greet us. Seeing him standing there reminded me of a king standing on the balcony of his castle. He had been encouraged by many of my mother's family to sell the house and leave. Then we wouldn't have to live near Devin's family. But my father stubbornly said, "No, no man is going to run my family off our land and out of our home." There he stood, with a look of confidence that his castle and family would not only bind together, but survive the attack from the enemy camp.

I walked toward the house, though I wanted to run. Still not steady on my feet, I simply walked as fast as I could toward the front door. The moment I got in arm's reach of my Daddy, he gave me a big hug and asked me how I felt. I assured Dad that I felt great, even as I stepped into the door of the house. Mother was sitting on the couch with several pillows propping up her arm. I tried to ignore that sight. It pained my insides that Mother wore metal bars to connect her arm together. Then I slowly walked into the living room.

Many of my family and loved ones had come to the house to welcome me home. Then I saw Jarvis, my second cousin on Mother's side of the family. He was standing beside Stacy James, my next door neighbor. I walked over to Jarvis who said the same thing he'd said to me for fourteen years, "Hey, cuz." He looked right at me like nothing had happened and I was okay. We then talked a blue streak until I was pulled away to speak to other people. Jarvis and I had played together when we were younger. He always encouraged me when I was down, even when no one else noticed that I needed it. Talking to Stacy, I could tell this ordeal had made a great impact on her. We had spent the last seven years playing together almost every day of the week. She had been a good friend to me. Most importantly, she stood for Christian values that we both held close to our hearts.

Alex and Ben spoke to me that day, but in a way, they kept their distance. They knew that I was far from being back to my old self. For Ben and Alex, that devastating day in my life had been a tragedy that they had been forced to live with, perhaps even in ways more difficult than those I had to face. They were forced to deal with all the emotional anguish, tears, and feelings of helplessness while watching Mother and me suffer.

Candy really had not been given the time to fall apart or to deal much with her feelings of helplessness. Despite not being able to help Mother and me with our struggles, she had to come through for Daddy. There was no question as to who was going to hold down the fort at home. Daddy turned to Candy to be there for Ben and Alex. She was also expected to take the responsibility of responding to the hometown and divulging our family's response to the shooting.

I found out the next day that a neighbor, Sis Horton, had taken the shooting to heart. She cooked a good southern meal and brought it over to the house. Daddy was overwhelmed with gratitude. Candy and Daddy were both so busy, the family didn't have big meals very often.

The physical battle had overwhelmed me so much that I had put my emotions on the back burner. It only took one look at Mother to see that she still had not faced the harsh truth about what had happened to us. In some ways, she looked like a zombie, dazed and unable to feel any sense of reality. She appeared to be in a deep state of denial.

I tried not to focus on all the feelings that were surging through me. Nor did I dwell on where my family stood concerning the incident. I tried my best to appear strong both physically and emotionally so that I could enjoy the moment at hand. I was home, surrounded by both family and loved ones. This was one of the best moments of my life. If I had been asked the question, is there anything I wanted, I would have had to say no. The fact that I was alive and home seemed to vanquish all other thoughts from my heart. It was getting late in the day, and Lynne saw that I was getting tired. Lynne came over and put his arm around me as though to tell me we better get ready to head back to his house.

Just before we walked out the door, Daddy walked up to me and said, "Lisa, there is something special I have been waiting to tell you. Your classmates at school did a fundraiser by having a dance while you were in the hospital. I have saved the money for you to do something special with; it was a little over three hundred dollars."

I froze for a moment like a deer in headlights as I tried to grasp how much my friends at school had given me such unconditional support. Daddy hugged me as he saw how overwhelmed I was by the news. I finished saying my goodbyes and soon had to go back to the place that I knew as my temporary home.

Soon, while living with Lynne and Dixie, I began to adjust to life outside the hospital walls. Yet, around the clock, I was on a breathing machine and another machine that cleaned out my trachea. My feeding machine, which was connected to my g-tube, seemed to be on twenty-four hours a day. I went to sleep with it feeding me. In my sleep, the drip would stop, but once I awoke the bag would fill back up. I had to push a machine around with me almost all day long. I had been there for only a couple of weeks when they arranged for me to start homeschooling. Kathy Conn was set up as my teacher. She came out for a couple of hours during the afternoon. She was a Christian who often took time to encourage me. She reminded me that with the Lord strengthening me every step of the way, I was going to be okay. Her words of inspiration meant a lot to me. My focus on school work was not an easy task. The writing assignments I did with my left hand, and this was a big challenge. My mind had a hard time zeroing in on math, English, and history. I still had so many questions about what was going to happen to me next.

Despite the questions racing through my mind, Lynne wouldn't let me be lazy. He was not the type to let grass grow under his feet or *mine*, by allowing me to lie around all day. He exercised my mind by going over some of my school work. Or he took me for an evening walk. The evening walks became something I highly enjoyed. It reminded me that I was in the country, not in some big city. After about a month at Lynne's, we had to go back to Houston for a check up.

THE JOURNEY I
HAD TO FINISH

I was so excited on the first Sunday that I was able to go to church. Caroline and Rex were visiting for the weekend, which made going to church that much more special. We called Aunt Bernice and Uncle Doil and invited them to come spend this special day with us. That morning could not come soon enough for me. I was so eager to go with Mother to our church. There were so many people I that wanted to hug and thank for all their prayers, cards, and gifts. And most importantly, I wanted to again make that trip that I started to make on January 5, 1986, so to feel that I had completed a small journey.

At last the sun appeared over the tall pine trees, signaling a new morning, and I awoke, eager for the day to begin. I told Dixie and Lynne that I was awake and ready for my breathing treatments and medicine. Lynne entered my room with a big smile on his face and greeted me with his good morning speech.

Lynne, like my mother, always started off the day with a smile and a word about how wonderful or beautiful a day it was going to be. Dixie soon joined us. Wearing her cheery smile, she asked me what I wanted to wear to church. I replied that I wanted to wear my favorite pant suit. Lynne began my treatments. I, of course, had to do my part. I was so eager to go to church that I cooperated wholeheartedly. We finally got through with the medical tasks and then got dressed for church.

We drove up to Mother and Dad's where we were all going to meet before church. I could hardly wait for the car to stop. I was anxious to go inside to see everyone. Aunt Bernice and Uncle Doil soon arrived. My mind was consumed with the adventure we were about to go on. The day that I was shot, only a few people had tried to protect me. But today, I had a whole host of family members that were going to be beside me.

Finally the moment came when our caravan was on its way to church. The dirt road was dry for a change. The moment we drove on to the pavement, memories started coming back to me. When we reached the top of the hill, I looked over at the shoulder of the farm market road. I could still see the tracks we had made. They had been deeply embedded in the mud that tragic day. I kept trying to block out that day from my mind. No matter how hard I tried, the memories were still there. Before I realized it, we were arriving in front of the church and our caravan began to stop. I wasn't sure why, but stopping there made memories pour through me like a deluge of heavy rainfall.

It was Sunday morning, and the little Macedonian Church parking lot was full. I could see that the worshipers were already inside and the service had started. Here is where my nightmare had begun. Mother walked up to me as I exited my car and said, "Lisa, Lynne thinks we need to go inside and say thank you to everyone for what they did that day. I agreed with him that we should. Are you up to it?" My first thought was, how could I say no? But it wasn't something I had prepared myself to do. I had mentally prepared myself to speak to everyone at our church, but not this one.

I took a deep breath and nodded my head yes. Mother and I began walking toward the church doors. With each step we took, I thought about how pitiful we both must look. And we were about to stand in front of a church to speak to the members. Rex escorted us to the church and opened the door for us. Mother and I stepped inside the front door and then into the atrium. Brother Howell was behind the pulpit speaking when he noticed Mother and me. He was speechless for a moment. The entire congregation, upon hearing the doors open, had turned to face us.

All eyes were upon us as Mother took the opportunity to say, "Brother Howell, we would just like to say something."

Brother Howell said, "Yes, Reba, and Lisa, you may speak." We walked down the aisle, while everyone watched each step. I wanted so badly to reach out and hold Mother's hand. However, that was impossible since both of our right arms were in slings. Walking on my blind side, Mother made me feel as though I was making the walk all alone. Slowly we made it to the front of the church and turned to face the congregation. Mother, now standing on my right side, started to deliver her speech. She, of course, gave praise to the Lord for our being alive. Then she offered a most heartfelt thank you. Then she looked at me, silently letting me know it was my turn to speak. I took a deep breath and attempted to speak. But my voice cracked. I struggled to speak so that they could hear my words. "I just want to say thank you for everything ya'll did for us that day. It was because of people like ya'll who prayed and believed, that my life was saved. I can never express how thankful I am for what ya'll did that Sunday morning. I praise God that I am alive. Thank ya'll!" I looked at Mother to let her know that I had finished speaking.

We both started to walk back down the aisle when Sammy stood to his feet. This was the man who had cradled me in his arms on that horrible day. He had held me until the ambulance had arrived. I stopped in the aisle listening as Sammy spoke, his voice choking up.

"Lisa, I'm so glad you stopped by today."

Then I heard Mother speak. "Lisa, do you know who this is?"

I quickly replied, "How could I ever forget?" Then I looked in Sammy's eyes and said, "Thank you, especially." I opened my arms to receive a hug. We were both holding back tears as we embraced. As I felt his arms around me, I closed my eyes. I could hear his voice, again. Not the voice of today, but the words he had spoken to me on that day. Words of faith and hope and I'd held on to them for dear life. We only embraced for a moment, yet it meant so much to me.

After embracing Sammy, I noticed that Virginia had risen to hug Mother. As I stood watching them, with joy bubbling over, I noticed a line forming. I knew then that everyone in the small church wanted a hug and a personal moment, to express their love and gratitude. In my heart, I wanted to hug everyone, too. It was *this* congregation that witnessed the day that changed my life forever. They were the ones crying as it happened and kept me lifted up before the Lord. We left the church with smiles on our faces and thankfulness in our hearts.

We were walking to the car when we saw Austin walking across the road. Mother and I knew instinctively that we had to go speak to him. We walked right past the cars and met Austin, where he embraced both of us. He had one arm around

Mother's neck and the other arm around my neck. Tears were streaming down his face. His words were so simple. "My Girls, my girls, you're alive, my girls." After a few moments he stepped back and told us we'd never know how much it meant to him to see us this day. Looking into Austin's kind, compassionate face, tears welled up in my eyes. This made it impossible for me to speak, so Mother spoke on our behalf. Choked up herself, she thanked Austin for his help on that infamous day. We stood there in the presence of God Almighty, with thanksgiving and joy leaping inside our hearts. I regained my composure as I wiped a few tears from my eyes, and I thanked Austin from the bottom of my heart. Mother and I then stepped away and walked back to the caravan.

We were now on our way to Pineland Church. Once back in the car, I was glad we stopped at Macedonia. Despite how difficult it was for me, deep inside, it had been a good thing. Once I had stepped inside the church, most of the bloody memories had faded. It was as though the silver lining in a dark cloud shined through a moment, sweeping away the memories. The rest of the way to our church, I just reminded myself of the main fact: I was alive. The thought that made my heart leap for joy was that I was going to complete my journey this day. A journey, which to me, had a significant meaning.

I come from a very competitive family who hates to lose at anything. Even losing a game of horse shoes or dominoes makes us irate for the rest of the day. I wanted this day to prove something to the devil himself and to Devin. I wanted to prove that I would not be defeated, because the word of God says in I John 4:4, "Ye are of God, little children and have overcome them: because greater is he that is in me, than he that is in the world."

We arrived at the church e and took some pictures. The moment I stepped out of the car, excitement rose inside me. It was so great that I wanted to leap for joy. Here I stood at Pineland Life Christian Teaching Center Church. I had started out on January 5, 1986, for this destination. This had been the longest trip I had ever made coming to church. Inside, the service had already begun. We all took our seats. Everyone in the church was smiling as we began to praise the Lord. We had sung three or four songs when Lynne rose from his seat. He walked up to the front of the church and began singing with our praise and worship leader. After we finished that song, the leader stepped back from the microphone so that Lynne could speak.

Lynne praised the Lord for such a wonderful day. He then explained how he had stayed with me in the hospital, and was taking care of me now. He got emotional as he said, "Lisa is a miracle, and I have seen it with my own eyes. I just wanted to praise God for what He has allowed me to witness." After speaking from his heart and singing praise with the praise and worship leader, Lynne returned to his seat in the congregation. The services then went on as usual, in which I enjoyed hearing the Word of God.

When the last 'amen' dismissed the service, I faced the people as they approached Mother and me. I could tell they all wanted to show their most heartfelt gratitude for our appearance. These people had spent many endless hours in prayer on behalf of Mother's life and for mine. The ladies of this congregation had been dear friends to my mother as long as I could remember. After I thought I had hugged everyone, I noticed someone at the back of the church that I had left out. It was Sister Dee, whom I had known since I was knee-high to a grasshopper. She spread her arms open wide as I walked toward her. Tears welled up in her eyes as she began to express how thankful to the Lord she was that I was alive. As Sister Dee embraced me, she hugged me so tight that her shoulder rubbed against my trachea.

So tight, in fact, that my trachea had been pushed back in my neck. The pain made me cringe and I wondered what I was going to do. After Sister Dee had finished hugging me and expressing to me how much she loved me, I turned away so that no one would notice. I reached up with my hand and felt my trachea. It was mashed almost all the way inside my neck. I took a quick breath and with my hand pulled it back out. Now it was back where it was supposed to be. After that, I didn't hug anyone else so tightly. Shortly after that incident, our family departed the church, headed home in our caravan.

Arriving at home, we all prepared for Sunday dinner. Caroline had planned and prepared it for the family. Everyone sat around the table and the feast began. Lynne hooked me up to my feeding machine. Mother sat in front of me with her arm propped up with pillows. Still sitting in the living room, she and I had more things on our minds than feasting at the table. We wanted to discuss how happy everyone was to see us doing so well. As I sat there with my family, a scripture kept echoing in my ears: "The devil comes to kill, steal and destroy." I knew that on January 5, 1986, he had come to kill me. But because of prayer to my heavenly Father, that did not happen. This day for my family and me was like a celebration of victory over the devil. I tried not to think about what lay ahead. Instead, I just wrapped myself in the joy of the moment.

Just when I thought the day could not get any better Caroline called me into the dining room. I pushed my feeding machine and walked in there as Caroline also called Lee into the room. Caroline had something in her hand as she began to tell me a story. Lee was a member of a motorcycle club and they had told the organization about what had happen to me. The club had sent Lee not just a shirt he had coming but also one to me with a letter of sympathy. Caroline put the shirt in Lee's hand and said don't you have something to say to your Aunt Lisa. Lee took the shirt out of the bag and with a big smile handed it to me only to say if you don't want it Lisa I will take it. Caroline quickly got on to Lee, but it only made me laugh as I said, "Maybe one day Lee I will give it to you." It was a long sleeved, beautiful shirt which I was very honored to have received. Lee gave me a hug as he spoke gently the words "I love you Lisa" the best he could with tubes coming out of me as I looked into his tender eyes. He stood so young to have to try and grip everything that had happened. I looked over to the corner of the room and saw Brittany watching. I see in her eyes that she was hurting from deep within. Lee and Brittany were always right under Ben, Alex and my feet. We never did anything without including them to tag alone. I wanted at that moment just to turn back time and be getting off the school bus and running to play with Lee and Brittany. During their spring break, they would always come see us and wait anxiously for us to get home from school. Our running and playing often carried us to the pasture to make forts and huts out of bricks Daddy had laying around. We would take sticks straw, leaves, hay or what ever we got our hands on to make a roof. Those years of running and playing were going to always be special to me as the future seemed uncertain. I stood and left the room to go put my shirt up only to find my self in Candy and my bedroom crying. I was crying and did not want anyone to know as I thought about the what ifs. I finally pulled myself together with a sincere prayer. "Dear Lord if I am never able to run and play again please help Lee and Brittany remember the good old days" Lord please take their pain away help them to understand what has happen and Lord help them forgive" "Oh Dear God never let them forget how much I love them" After I cried out these words and wiped my tears I returned to family gathering trying to act brave and confident.

THE TORNADO

The time for another trip to Houston arrived too soon. In order to make the journey easier on me, we spent the night in a hotel. The next morning, Lynne, Dixie, and I headed to see my doctors. We were all happy to hear a good report. I was told that I looked and sounded great. We saw Doctor Stein, Doctor Poke, and Doctor Mills. I had only one question for them—when was the next operation? I was told that it would be a while. I still needed some internal healing from my prior surgeries and gunshot wounds. They wanted to give me even more time for that to occur. This news put a smile on my face and a spring in my step. After we saw all the doctors, we headed for home. It was a long drive, and I slept most of it lying down in the back seat.

Lynne and Dixie did all they could to make me feel relaxed and at home. They allowed me to see my immediate family as often as possible. Their biggest challenge was trying to make me feel safe. There was a part of me that feared Devin would break out of jail and come after me again. The fact that I had lived when Devin wanted me dead haunted me the most at night.

Many times, I requested Dixie to lie beside me in my bed until I fell asleep. Dixie never hesitated to help me feel safe. Lynne would always assure me that he was going to protect me, no matter what. He assured me that no one was coming after me.

It was now April, and I continued to enjoy living with Lynne and Dixie. I was progressing so well that I planned to go spend the day at home with my immediate family. I heard that Caroline had come down with Lee, Brittany, and Luke. I was looking forward to spending the day with my niece and nephews. I knew I would not be able to run, play, or ride horses with them as usual on the farm, but I was still excited beyond words. Daddy and Brittany, my niece arrived at Lynne's house right after I had finished receiving my breathing treatment, medication, and feeding in the g-tube. Brittany hesitated momentarily, then walked over and gave me a hug. I thought she was still trying to get used to seeing all the tubes, scars, and my weird-looking left eye. I asked her to walk back with me to the bedroom so I could get something.

We were in the bedroom for a moment when Brittany looked at me and said, "Lisa, did you know a tornado struck our trailer house?"

Stunned, I gasped for a breath said, "What did you say?"

"Yes, a tornado ripped the roof off. A tornado hit Kilgore. I think it killed some people."

I managed to ask, "Brittany, are ya'll ok?"

"Yes, but the thing almost killed us." Brittany spoke in a whisper. It was as though she didn't want anyone but me to hear what she was telling. But I could feel that she was still in a state of shock. The look in her eyes was like looking in the mirror as she told me of the horrible tornado. I could almost see the fear of death still hanging over her head. Brittany continued telling me all the things that happened, but her words seem to fade into the distance. Then I recalled a verse in the Bible that says, "The devil comes to kill, steal, and destroy." Then a cold chill came over me. It hit me like a ton of bricks. I suddenly realized that I was not the only one in the family that the devil was trying to kill. He had tried to kill Rex and Caroline's entire family that night.

I found out later that no one really wanted me to know how bad the tornado had been in Kilgore. But I persisted with questions until I got some answers. I was overwhelmed with joy when I realized that our family was pulling together once again! Ron, the carpenter in the family, led an expedition to replace the roof on the trailer house. Carl and Daddy also went there the next day to offer support and help. Daddy couldn't stay long because he had to return home to tend to Mother. I could tell that Mother was still in a state of denial. It was as though I could hear the devil roaring like a lion in the distance, and I was walking through the back side of the desert. Trembling, I began to pray, "Lord, help Caroline. I know she is trying not to make me worry. Lord, she needs your strength. I pray for the Lord to help Lee, Brittany, and Luke feel safe again in your arms." I had faith that God could protect us through his power, although physically and mentally I didn't feel all that protected or safe.

THE DARK SECRETS

A few months had elapsed since I left the hospital. Things seemed to be going great for me in many ways. But one day, everything I had going for me shattered. Like the waves on the sea shore my joy crashed, sweeping away all my confidence like it swept the sand on the shores. Lynne and I were going to feed the cows, and I was driving across the pasture. There, Lynne started a serious conversation with me. He began explaining how the trial against Devin was coming up. And the district attorney had some important questions for me to answer. Just the thought of talking to lawyers made my heart seem to stop beating. Lynne went on to explain what he needed to know. "Lisa, you and Devin had become close friends. We all know that. What we really need to know is, the details about *every time* you saw him. Did you ever see Devin, when no one else, like your parents, knew about it?" I began to slow the truck down as all my limbs went numb and my heart beat seemed to fade away. Before I could answer, Lynne explained, "All of this information is going to come out in court.

Our lawyers need to know about it before then." After that he paused, giving me the opportunity to come clean.

Tears welled up in my eyes as I stuttered the words, "But, Lynne, I can't tell my parents. They will be so disappointed in me."

He assured me that my parents would understand. I had to remember that they loved me and would support me, no matter what had happened. The most important words at that moment, that Lynne could have spoken, he said so eloquently. "Lisa, you know you can trust me, that I will be beside you, when you tell your parents and lawyers." Hearing those words gave me the assurance that everyone would understand. I stopped the truck, in the middle of Lynne's pasture. There, I began telling him about, what I had thought at one time, were priceless memories.

The first episode that I shared with Lynne was also the biggest heartache, for I knew how much Ben detested Devin. Devin asked me at school if we could meet somewhere private and visit. I agreed to go horseback riding and meet him at a place in the woods, Monkey Tree Island. This was the nickname that the neighborhood kids had given to a unique place in the woods, by a creek. Saddling the horse that Saturday morning, I was very nervous, not knowing what to expect from Devin. But once I had saddled Misty, I headed out without any interruptions. As I came up to my destination, I saw Devin had already arrived. He appeared to be eagerly awaiting my appearance. He greeted me by helping me tie up my horse. He then walked over to his motorcycle and pulled two sodas out of a paper sack. Having eaten with me so many times at school, he had known and chosen my favorite Sunkist. We sat down on the ground and visited for a little over two hours. We talked endlessly it seemed, about family, friends, and school.

My attraction for Devin happened almost over night. I wanted so much to be open about it, but I was torn between my own growing affection for him and my family loyalty. It was no secret that Ben did not like Devin whatsoever. Their mutual dislike for one another placed tension on any relationship Devin and I tried to maintain. I desired my brother's approval so much that I often believed that with time, he would come to like Devin. Devin wanted to be my boyfriend so much, he was willing to put aside his differences with Ben. Unfortunately, as long as Ben's dislike mounted against Devin, it made our contact outside of birthday parties and school very limited. But that day was the beginning of my believing in Devin in a special way. I thought no one could ever take that away.

Just as I finished sharing that story, Lynne asked, "Lisa, is there anything else you need to tell me?" He had the most sympathetic voice. I had never heard a more understanding one come from any father. He was trying his best to help me feel relaxed and confident enough to confide my dark secrets, the things that only Devin and I had shared with each other. I inhaled deeply and told Lynne the next event that came to mind. This one really made me hang my head in shame. I had lied to my Daddy, and it was breaking my heart.

Excitement was building at school because another birthday party was coming up. Some of our classmates had got together and were going to have a skating party. The anticipation at school was the possibility of getting a date. Many girls were being asked out for dates to the party. I wasn't giving this a whole lot of thought. I wasn't even thinking much whether or not Devin would be coming to the party. The day the invitations were handed out, Devin asked me to be his date at the party. Of course I was surprised by this. I had already expressed to him that I was too young to date.

I hesitated about saying no, but that was going to be my response. That is, until Devin started unloading his master plan. "Lisa, no one has to know but me and you. I will meet you at the party and just hang out with you there. It will be like, we are just being friends. Your parents will just be dropping you off for the party and won't be there to pay any attention to us." After hearing this plan, I thought it actually might work. Maybe we could meet at the party and have a good time and it wouldn't hurt anything.

I smiled, though fear tugged at my insides, and I said, "Yes, I'll be your date." The look on Devin's face was priceless, his expression as though he had just won a million dollars. The rest of the week, I didn't tell anyone what Devin and I had planned for Friday night at the birthday party. I knew that with my luck, if I told anyone it would get back to Ben. That would mean trouble for me.

Friday finally arrived. I was so excited, thinking about what it would be like to have a date. School that day seemed to go by so slowly. All my friends and I talked about was the birthday party that night. Almost all my friends bragged about who their date would be. I kept my mouth shut. School finally came to a close, and I took my usual long bus ride. All the time, I was looking forward to getting ready for the party. Mother, Dad, and Alex were going to take me to the party. Then they would pick me up after it was over. The time to leave for the party brought the flutter of butterflies to my stomach.

The thought kept racing through my mind, "What have I gotten myself into with Devin? Would he take this to mean I wanted to be more than just his real good friend? More than someone to hang out with at school?" Well, whatever it meant, I would soon find out. We loaded up in the car and headed off to the party. Driving up in the driveway could not have been a more uncomfortable situation. To my chagrin, Devin was sitting on his motorcycle, outside the skating rink, waiting for my arrival. I had the car door half opened before Daddy even had the car stopped. I was so nervous and scared that he would ask if Devin was waiting outside for me. I quickly said goodbye to everyone in the car and shut the door with no hesitation. They said bye and have fun. Then they left.

I swiftly walked toward the door to the skating rink, trying not to even look Devin's direction. To my embarrassment, Devin walked right up beside me and started talking while he escorted me to the door and opened it for me. All I could think about was that my parents were watching. They would probably have some questions for me when I got home.

Inside, we said hello to everyone while we made our way to put on our skates. The night from that point on seemed to go by so fast. We all skated to the country and western music playing over the loud speakers.

As the night passed, though, I began to notice that none of my good friends were speaking to me. They all stood back, at a distance, as though they weren't sure how to talk to me what with Devin standing right beside me. The party was winding down when Devin and I started to talk about our relationship. I expressed my concerns to Devin. Our families were not best friends, and I even asked him what his parents' opinions were about us. Devin said his daddy had told him to be careful about what he was getting into with me. But his mother, on the other hand, had no reservations, saying she liked me. I tried explaining to Devin that according to my parents, I was still too young to date and there was no changing their minds.

But then, as we spoke, there was a lump in my throat. I had something hard to say to him. "Devin, it's not that I haven't had fun tonight. But, there is something I didn't like about tonight. I've never been on a date before. Why haven't any of my friends spoken to me tonight? You are the only person I have had a conversation with during the whole party. All my other friends did was say hi when we walked into the room. That was it. If this is what dating is all about, I don't like it. I don't want to lose all my other friends just because I am starting to hang out with you." Devin assured me that they just hadn't had time to adjust to me and him being side-by-side for a whole party. He told me to just relax and give my friends time to come around. Everything would be okay.

We agreed that my friends were a small part of the equation compared to my parents. The party came to a close shortly after our conversation. Devin saying goodnight in a room full of people was special only in the way he looked into my eyes. It was as though we were the only ones in the room. He gently let go of my hand. The way he looked at me made me melt inside. I felt like I was the most beautiful and important person in the world. In that moment, he seemed like a person I wanted to get to know in a more personal way. Surely my parents would give him a chance.

I rode home that night not saying much to Mother and Dad except that I had a good time. I was so thankful they didn't have an avalanche of questions for me. Alex just talked about where they went out to eat and so forth. Once we arrived at home, I went straight to bed with a hidden smile on my face. I thought I had pulled it off, getting to be with Devin.

Sunrise came and time for Mother's usual way of waking up everyone. She popped open the shades and asked, "How is your fat this morning?" This was a country way of saying "it's time to rise and shine no sleeping late in this house." We, as usual, tried to ignore the sun rays flooding through the windows. Once mother announced that breakfast was ready, we all crawled out of our beds and started to get dressed.

I was walking into the bathroom to brush my teeth when Alex came rushing out of his room. "Lisa, we got to talk, it's important." I could tell by the look on his face that he was not pulling my leg. So I stopped to hear what was on his mind. "Lisa, you are in big trouble about last night's party. Mother and Dad came back before the party was over. They stood outside looking in the windows where no one could see them. They saw you and Devin skating together and holding hands. Dad plans on asking you about it this morning. You better have a good excuse ready for him."

My heart stopped beating. I was so scared. What was I going to do? I thanked Alex for giving me a heads up on what to expect. What was I going to say to Daddy? All I knew was, I was going to say *anything* but the truth. There was just no way I would tell Daddy that Devin had asked me to be his date at the party. After brushing my teeth, I slowly walked into the kitchen.

Sure enough, the moment Daddy saw me, he walked over to me and asked, "Lisa did you and Devin have a date last night at the skating party?"

With my stomach tied in knots, I barely got the word out, "No." I made sure I didn't make eye contact with Daddy.

He then asked, "Then why did you spend all your time at the party with Devin?"

"Daddy, he was at the party. So we just hung out together and talked." My answers seemed to satisfy him, but I felt so rotten inside for not telling Daddy the whole truth. I decided to forgot breakfast and go on outside. Suddenly I had lost my appetite.

After I had shared that most painful memory with Lynne, I expected to hear him reproach me and tell me how wrong I was for not telling Daddy the truth. Instead, Lynne explained that nothing I had done gave Devin the right to shoot me. He shared even more with me. Devin's actions were not only a crime, but an immoral act. The more Lynne talked, the better I began to feel inside. He understood my heart despite my past. Inside, however, I knew there was more I had to say. I just hoped that he would continue to be supportive and understanding. Then Lynne paused for a moment. This gave me an opportunity to reveal more of my secret. After taking another deep breath, I told him there was one more episode I had to tell him about.

The trust I felt for Devin seemed to grow to new heights rapidly. I began to have a new feeling deep inside that someone just needed to believe in him. My belief that he had basically a good character seemed to overshadow anything bad that I had heard about Devin. I will never forget that day at school when Devin said that he had to tell me something important. I remember holding my breath, wondering what he was going to say that was so important. He then told me that lunch period wasn't long enough for him to tell me, so would I please do the unthinkable and sneak out of my house that night to talk to him? He remembered that I had told him that Candy would be gone until late that night.

At first I told him no. That didn't satisfy him. I made the mistake of looking into his deep blue eyes and was swept away in the moment. We made plans to meet that night around nine-thirty or ten. Devin left me with a smile on his face so wide that no one could wipe it off, but I left with fear griping my insides. I feared that we might be caught. If so, I would be in serious trouble with my parents. Despite the fear, a part of me was curious about what Devin was going to tell me. I didn't confide in anyone the plans that we had made. I was too scared that it would get back to Ben.

The day seemed to pass so slowly. At last the sun rested behind the tall pine trees and darkness slowly settled in. I went to bed that night as usual, but I only pretended to be asleep. I waited with much anticipation for everyone else to go to bed. A couple of hours later I heard Devin at my window. I jumped out of bed and slipped on my pants and shoes. Fully dressed now, I crept out the front door. Part of me was excited to see Devin, while another part was still gripped with fear. We decided to get far enough from the house so no one could hear us talking. We walked down the dirt road, laughing and talking about just everyday things. About half way down the dirt road, we came upon Devin's motorcycle.

He asked me to go for a ride with him, but I refused. I reminded him we didn't have much time. It was so late, and Candy could be coming home anytime now. I wasn't sure what to be more scared of if Candy caught us, what she would do to Devin, or me. Mother had stayed up so late reading her Bible that it made us late getting started. We decided it would be better for us to start walking back to the house. Without warning Devin put his arm around me as we walked side by side.

As we neared my home, Devin began to open his heart to me. "Lisa, I wanted to tell you tonight how much I care for you. I have never felt this way in my whole life. I believe I have fallen in love with you. I want to see you more often, more than just at school." He kept talking softly to me, his words going deep into my heart. Actually hearing Devin open up to me like this made me nervous. Rushing through my mind was this thought: *How do I actually feel about Devin? Yes I trust him, but I am not sure if*

I'm in love. Fortunately for me, he didn't come that night to ask me questions. He came to pour out his heart. When we got back beside the porch, it was time to say goodnight. He looked into my eyes as though he was reaching my inner soul with such love and compassion. Then he asked, "May I kiss you?"

It was so romantic as I looked at Devin standing there in the moonlight. I was amazed that he had asked permission. I enthusiastically replied yes.

Devin looked down into my face and said, "I've never kissed a girl before. I'm not sure I know how."

I smiled and said, "Close your eyes and think about how they do it in the movies." Devin closed his eyes and leaned down to kiss me. When our lips met, my heart seemed to stand still. Devin kissed me with tenderness and kindness, more than I had ever felt.

After the kiss, he not only smiled with joy, but he said, "Thank you."

We said goodnight and I eased back into the house as Devin faded away in the moonlight. I went to bed but did not sleep at all. I was asking myself a million questions. What had I gotten myself into? Were we really in love? What was I going to do now? The one thing that became real to me was that Devin had serious feelings for me. But the feelings were *not mutual.* Therein lay a huge problem.

I could no longer speak after I had told Lynne about my worst act of all. I wondered what my heavenly Father was going to say about my transgressions, as well as my earthly father. Lynne took my hand and said, "Lisa, look at me. There is one important fact that has to come out in the open. No matter what the answer is you must be honest with me, okay? Did you and Devin have sex together?"

I quickly blurted out with deep conviction, "No! No! *I promise that never happened.*"

Lynne smiled. In his eyes I could see the relief as that of a father looking into the eyes of his own daughter. Lynne seemed to sense that I couldn't handle anymore questions now. So he smiled and said, "Come on, let's go feed the cows before dark." I drove on to the barn, trying to forget about what I had brought out in the open. I knew the meeting with Daddy and the lawyers was just a few days away.

TALKING TO THE LAWYERS

The time came, much too soon, that I was going to have to face the music and talk to my father. The thought of how my Daddy was going to take the news overrode every other thought. I had finished my morning breathing treatments, feeding machine, and medications, when I went into the den. I waited there for everyone to arrive. This was going to be my first time to meet the two men, the district attorney and assistant district attorney, who would be handling the case. Daddy, Mother, and Ben arrived first and joined me in the house. Then the lawyers arrived.

As I thought about all the things we had to talk about, my heart almost stood still. The district attorney began the discussion as we all gathered in the den of Lynne's and Dixie's home. He shared with me his most heartfelt sympathy for what had happened to our family. I noticed as he spoke that he kept looking at me. I could sense that he wanted me to feel comfortable with him. He wanted me to know that he did have a heart of kindness for victims of violent crime. The district attorney explained how he wanted to hear each of us give an account of what happened on that day. Mother was first to report what she could remember about the shooting. Listening to her speak was not easy for me. It was as though she was in a daze as she recalled what had occurred. For the first time in her life, she was not descriptive, but rather straight to the point. Her tone of voice remained level. What she was saying, perhaps she felt, did not carry any weight or put stress on her emotions. I could tell Mother was still in a state of denial. Perhaps this was all just a bad dream and she was going to wake up at any time now. Daddy sat right beside her, listening intently as she spoke. His face registered pain with each word that she uttered, as though someone was putting a dagger in his heart. It seemed to me that it was taking all the strength his weary body could muster to resist breaking into uncontrollable tears. Daddy never looked at me. Would looking into my eyes be more than he could bear?

After mother had finished, Ben was asked to tell his story next. He spoke with anger coloring his deep-toned voice, outlining for the lawyers what happened as he saw it. Ben gave more details than we could. He was able to describe the scene that Mother and I could not. He explained what happened after we were shot. He painted a picture of blood and screams for help. He related how Mother and I bled profusely while lying on the cold, wet ground that morning. The lawyers wrote frantically on their note pads. Then the big question came up—what type relationship did Devin and I have with each other? Everyone in the room seemed to take a long, questioning look at me. I knew that this very same question was in all their minds. Before I had time to answer, Lynne spoke up. He suggested that Ben step outside while I answered the personal questions.

The lawyers agreed, thinking that it would make me feel more comfortable answering all the questions. Ben went out in the front yard and began to toss some baskets while we continued inside. All the attention was focused on me as I began answering the attorney's questions. I explained that my family already knew that Devin and I were just neighborhood friends. We had become acquainted at school. After I had explained all of that, I paused. I needed assurance that my Daddy would understand all this. Then I took one last look at Lynne. With trembling voice I began to explain about the events that my father and mother knew nothing about. I revealed to the lawyers, Mother, Dad, and Dixie everything that I had shared with Lynne earlier that week. I was so afraid that I would never be able to look at my Daddy in the same way again. It could never be the same after I shared my involvement with Devin with everyone. Despite how much I hated to, I forced myself to look over to my father. I could see the disappointment in his eyes. But, despite his shock and dismay, I saw that his eyes were still filled with love for his baby girl. I then looked over at Mother. She had nothing but shock written on her face, wondering just how all of this could have happened. But Mother's eyes showed her commitment. It was the same loyalty that made her stand in front of me that day, probably saving my life. Loyalty like that only comes from a heart filled with the unconditional love of God.

The lawyers stopped their questions and began looking through some papers they had gotten out of their briefcases. The district attorney looked at me and said, "Lisa we have papers here that say Devin pulled a gun on you at school. Can you tell us in your own words what happen that day? Lisa, also, tell us if there is anything you think we should know that lead up to that gun incident."

I was so relieved that we were going to talk about something Mother and Daddy knew all about. I related the incident as though I were reliving it all over again.

After Devin and I had skipped school together one day, this put the icing on the cake for my father. Devin had given me a promise ring and expressed his desire to one day be my husband. Daddy seemed to have had enough of trying to stay neutral with Devin. From that point on, he declared that there would be no contact between us. Daddy's contention was that at fourteen, I was too young to be that serious about any young man. At school all my friends noticed right away that Devin and I were not even speaking to one another. It seemed that my friends never did understand that I had no choice in the matter. Some of them encouraged me to talk to Devin despite what my parents thought. But in my heart I knew I could never go against my father's direct orders. Up to this point in our relationship, I had kept our special moments together a deep secret. Therefore, I really never felt I was disobeying my father. I just wasn't asking his permission about everything concerning my time with Devin.

The next few days turned into weeks. I felt like I was wading through knee-deep mud. Basketball wasn't even keeping my mind off the fact that I had let my parents down by skipping school. I regretted that I had hurt Devin unintentionally. All that mattered to me now was to prove my loyalty to my family. My love for my family far outweighed what I had felt for Devin.

School had become more and more difficult for me. I had to be careful to whom I spoke to. I never realized how hard it would be to make sure I didn't bump into Devin accidentally. About the time I had adjusted to not seeing Devin, I was surprised to see him one morning waiting for me beside my locker. "Devin what are you doing?" I asked. "Don't you know if we are caught talking we are both in a lot of trouble?"

"Lisa, I know, but I have to talk to you please, just for a minute before class starts," Devin pleaded.

"I am going to give these roses to Mrs. Calhoune," I said. "You wait over there near the door. I will be right back."

I had a bouquet of roses in my hand that I had picked for a teacher when I walked up to my locker.

I gave the roses to the teacher and tried to lift her spirits because I knew she was going through a difficult time. Returning back through the hall I guessed that Devin would make another plea for me to have a relationship with him. Devin was leaning up against the wall with a very sad but serious look on his face. I joined him and leaned up against the wall. I asked him, "What is it you want to say?"

"Lisa, I want us to be together," he said. "I miss you so much."

"Devin, I will not disobey my father. Our relationship as you knew it is over. It is time for us to go our separate ways. You can be loyal to your family, and I can be loyal to my family. Devin, neither one of our families like us being friends, much less anything else that could ever develop."

"Lisa, please…" he started.

I quickly cut Devin off by saying that it was almost time for the bell and I had to get on to class.

Devin snapped back, "No!" while at the same time grabbing my right wrist very tightly.

"Lisa, I have a gun," he said. "You are going to leave with me."

Then I felt something poking me in the stomach, so I looked down to see what it was. I noted his blue jean jacket wrapped around something pointing towards me. A shock wave went through my body at the thought of Devin pulling a gun on me. All that I could say was, "Oh, Lord, help me!"

With an angry smirk, Devin roared, "Don't talk that mess," and stuck the gun farther into my stomach. Then I became concerned about my friends who were standing in the hallway, waiting for class to start. I had to get Devin away from my friends. I certainly didn't want them to get caught in the middle of this. This was between Devin and me, not them.

With terror in my voice I said, "Let's go outside before a teacher sees us talking."

Devin did not let go of my wrist as we stepped outside the door onto the sidewalk. Once we got a little way down the sidewalk, I stopped walking and tried talking to Devin. Then I put my hand on the barrel of the gun, not wanting Devin to point it toward anyone but me.

"Devin what are you doing?" I asked.

Devin informed me that we would be leaving school together and going to Louisiana in his truck. "We will tell everyone that you are eighteen and we want to be married," he said. "If we are married, then your parents will have to let us stay together."

I was shocked that Devin had thought up such a dumb idea. I tried my best to reason with him. Inside, I was crying out to my heavenly Father to protect me and give me wisdom. Suddenly the bell rang and everyone started going into their classrooms. When people took their seats in the classroom, they could see Devin and me out the windows. This made me more nervous about what Devin might do. Then I saw Mrs. Buttons, the computer teacher, walking toward us on her way to the computer lab. I gave Mrs. Buttons a pained look, hoping she would realize that something was wrong. But she simply returned that look that she had so often given Devin and me. Her look meant that we had better get on to class before she had to reprimand us. As Mrs. Buttons passed by, I knew I was running out of time to handle this situation. Within minutes teachers would be asking us why we were not in class. I studied Devin carefully and thought maybe he really didn't have the heart to pull the trigger, so I decided to stand my ground.

"Devin, I don't know about you, but when I die I know I am going to heaven to face my heavenly Father," I said. "The last thing I want to do here on earth is disobey my parents, so I am not going to leave school with you. You will have to shoot me before I disobey my parents. Devin, do you hear me? I am not going to leave with you."

Devin looked into my eyes and said, "Okay, I get it. Now, take your hand off the gun barrel."

I replied, "Fine, do what you have to do," as I removed my hand from the gun.

Devin pressed the barrel of the gun directly into my stomach. I heard the unmistakable sound of a trigger being cocked. Devin looked me square in the eyes and said, "Ok, then if that is how you want it. Goodbye!" I took a deep breath, waiting for the sound of the gun being fired

What should I do next? Devin waited as I placed my hand back on the gun barrel. Then I started talking fast to him.

"How can you shoot me if you really love me?" I asked. "Is this the way you want to end it, with me dead and you spending the rest of your life in prison? If you pull the trigger, look how many classmates will be watching you from the windows. Devin, if we truly love each other, we can still be together. We just have to wait until I am out of high school. Devin, if you really love me, you can wait on me to be your wife."

As I talked, Devin's eyes began to fade and change back to their normal crystal blue. Tears began to well up in his eyes. This small sign gave me hope that I was getting through to him. I pleaded with Devin not to go through with it, but to walk me to class like he used to do, and then leave school himself. I promised Devin that if he would get rid of the gun, I wouldn't tell anyone he had threatened me with it. I explained how we could just put this whole thing behind us as one big mistake and never look back at it.

After pondering my words, Devin said, "Okay, Lisa."

Those two little words were music to my ears. I wasn't expecting a big apology or anything. I just wanted his cooperation at this point. Devin and I slowly walked toward the gym side by side. We had not gone far when I asked Devin if he would let go of my wrist. It was beginning to hurt because circulation had been cut off. Devin looked at me and said yes, but with a stern warning he added, "You better not run, or I will shoot you down in the back like a dog."

I managed to eek out, "Okay." In order for us to walk together, I had removed my hand from the gun barrel. This made me even more nervous. With each step, I strained to keep from screaming for someone to help me. I knew that if I could make it to the gym and convince Devin to leave, I would be safe. The gym seemed a hundred miles away. When we finally reached the gym, Devin didn't really have anything to say. He just looked into my frightened eyes, studying my reaction. Devin had a blank look on his face. I don't think that he knew what to do next now that his plan had failed. I sensed that I needed to reassure him that I wasn't going to report him. Now he had to leave campus with that gun before someone else caught him. After I gave Devin that reassurance and warning in the same breath, he said goodbye, and he walked toward the parking lot where his motorcycle was parked. I stood by the door of the gym shaking. I was afraid to move or turn my back to Devin. I wanted to make sure he wasn't going to change his mind.

I stood straight as a pole as tears began to stream down my face. I watched Devin walk to the parking lot. It was only when he had passed the gym that I felt certain he was going to leave. I ran into the gym, wrapped in complete terror.

The first person I saw was Coach Rice standing on the basketball court. I ran to him and told him all about what had just happened. Now that I was safe, my promise to Devin went out the window. I feared not telling anyone more than I feared keeping it a secret. Tears were racing down my face. My heart was beating very rapidly, and I was breathless from running so fast. I was barely able to speak. Coach Rice could tell by the look on my face that I had something very important to tell him. I finally got the words out, "Coach Rice, Coach Rice. Devin has a gun. He pulled a gun on—"

"Lisa, where is Devin now," he asked.

"He is past the gym walking toward the parking lot," I stuttered.

Coach Rice put his arm around me and ran with me over to the back of the gym. He then told the other two teachers in the gym to take care of me while he ran to the office. I sat on the basketball court with my back against the wall. Everything that had happen was beginning to crash down on me. I began to cry uncontrollably and scream, "No, no, no!" My teammates weren't sure what was going on, but they knew they had never seen me this way before. They tried to comfort me in their own ways.

My basketball teammates were the first to ask what had happened. When I told them and everyone else about Devin threatening me with a gun, they were speechless. But after it all soaked into their minds, they all begin to assure me that it was going to be okay. I continued to sit on the gym floor. Every muscle in my body was shaking with terror.

My teammates had circled around me, doing their best to make me feel safe. Then we heard Coach Rice calling my name. My teammates stepped aside as Coach Rice helped me to my feet. He insisted that I no longer had a reason to be scared, because Devin had left the campus and the police were on their way.

With his arm around my shoulder, Coach Rice said, "Come on, let's go to the nurse's station until your parents get here." Coach Rice asked Coach Smith to look after his class until he returned. He slowly walked with me out of the gym. Coach Rice's strong arm around my shoulder helped me stop shaking somewhat, but the tears still flowed down my face. We stepped into the hallway of the main building. There we saw Mr. Hill walking down the hall. The moment he saw my terrified expression, he stopped immediately and asked what was wrong. I couldn't bring myself to do anything but mutter, so Coach Rice spoke up on my behalf. Mr. Hill immediately assisted in walking us down the hallway. He asked Coach Rice if my parents had been notified about what had happened. After Coach Rice told him no, Mr. Hill said he would stop at the school office and call them himself.

Coach Rice walked me on to the nurse's station and laid me down on one of the cots. The nurse, Mrs. Hughes, inquired what in the world had happened to me. Coach Rice informed her of the incident. She noticed that my wrist was very red with marks on it. I was barely able to get the words out, but explained to her how Devin had grabbed my wrist so tightly that it cut off my circulation. Mrs. Hughes tried hard to calm me down. She told me to try and relax because my parents would be there soon. Time seemed to stand still as I lay on the cot in a fetal position, hoping any minute that Daddy and Mother would arrive. About twenty-five minutes passed from the time I had laid down to when I heard a familiar voice. I could hear Candy entering through the door yelling, "Where is my sister. Where is Lisa?" Mrs. Hughes pointed to the cot over in the corner. I was never so happy to see my sister in all my life. Standing behind Candy was an old friend from high school, Sherry Jacobs, who had a puzzled look on her face.

Candy ran over to me as I sat up on the cot. She wrapped her arms around me and said, "Lisa, it's okay. I am here. No one is going to hurt you. I promise, it's okay! Now tell me what all happened!"

I briefly told her how Devin had pulled a gun on me and tried to get me to leave the school with him. Even as Candy comforted me, I could hear anger in her voice. How dare he pull that gun on my baby sister! In a few minutes Daddy and Mother came into the room. I wondered what their reaction was going to be. Daddy had a stern and very concerned look on his face, whereas Mother seemed to have a look of disbelief. She didn't think that this could really be happening. Mother came over to us and told me not to worry any more. I was about to leave school with them. It was only a few more minutes until I was allowed to go home.

Being surrounded by family gave me a sense of protection to the point I was able to stop crying and shaking. I was composing myself in the hallway when Daddy asked Candy to go down and check on Alex.

While still in the hallway Daddy told me, "Lisa, we have to stop by the court house so you can make a statement for the police." Candy and Sherry were headed down the hall as Mother, Daddy, and I stepped onto the sidewalk to head for the car. We drove to short distance to the court house. When exiting the car, Mother said, "J. L., I know this may seem weird, but I am going to walk over to Brookshire Bothers Grocery to talk to Devin's mother."

Daddy opposed the thought of anyone speaking to Devin's family about this, but Daddy also knew when Mother thought she had to exercise the Christian response to a situation, there was no changing her mind. Daddy put his arm around me and said, "Come on Lisa, let's get this over with so we can go home."

Daddy and I entered the court house as Mother headed for Brookshire Brothers. We went upstairs to the second floor of the courthouse where we were escorted into a small room. A lady was sitting in front of a typewriter. The lady asked me to explain what had happened at school. I tried to block out of my mind that I had promised Devin I would keep it all a secret. Then I told the lady what had happened.

Daddy and I signed some papers after I had finished speaking, and then we were told we were free to leave. Mother was waiting for us when we reached the car. I wanted to know what Devin's mother had said. However, Daddy couldn't have cared less what any of them had to say. Mother reported that Devin's mother had left work early and wasn't there. Mother then asked if we had gotten everything taken care of in the courthouse. We told her yes, and Daddy explained that the police should be looking for Devin in a couple of hours. All I could think about on the way home was wishing the police would lock Devin up and throw away the key. When I got home, I was too scared to even go outside and shoot baskets. I remained in the house in a deep daze. After we had been home for a while, Daddy had a talk with me, explaining what would probably happen next to Devin.

Coach Lane, the principal, was going to speak with the Sheriff's department and press charges on behalf of Hemphill

I.S.D. The charges would be for bringing a gun to school and threatening my life. Daddy explained to me that this would teach him that he was not above the law of our town and had to be accountable for his behavior. Daddy explained how Devin's upbringing had taught him that he could run over other people with no respect for the law.

When Daddy left the room, I began to remember a day when I asked Devin rumors about his family were true regarding breaking the law and never getting in trouble. Devin's response put my mind at ease. I could still see him looking at me rather gently and saying, "Lisa, my family is like stories you have told me about your grandfather, great-uncles and great-aunts: they were good old boys and girls that had been in trouble with the law since the day they were knee-high to a grasshopper. Never meaning no one any harm, they just wanted to be allowed to have their own way when they come to a crossroad amongst neighbors." Devin told me stories how for generations, his family had not seen eye to eye with some of the neighbors. Devin that day looked straight in my eyes and said, "Lisa some people hold against me harsh feelings because of the deeds of my forefathers. Yes I have been in a few scrapes here and there, but I have never been thrown in jail or arrested." Devin reminded me that I had been taught to not judge a man by the past, because for all I knew, he had been forgiven. That day, I chose to believe only good things about Devin, no matter what anyone else had to say. But now, I had to face the harsh truth that Devin was willing to break the law. The day he faced Ben, Candy, and Sam, it wasn't a matter of self-defense, it was a crossroad, and he wanted to have his own way. I knew it was by the grace of God that I walked away that day unharmed physically, yet inside my heart was shattered.

THE WARNINGS WE
HAD ABOUT DEVIN

When I finished speaking to the lawyers, Daddy expressed his insight on Devin's mentality at that time. Daddy explained that he had heard in town that Devin was not acting normally. Rumors were that he was acting out in a way that they could not reason with him. We now saw everything in hindsight

The lawyers asked Daddy the question that seemed to be haunting everyone in town. "Mr. Barnett, was there anything that triggered this shooting?"

Daddy looked over at me, then turned to the lawyers and explained how we had already faced Devin pulling a gun on Ben, Candy, and Sam which he got off with self defense. Daddy said, "When Devin openly pursued an interest in Lisa, I put my foot down. I made it clear to Lisa I did not want her to see Devin no more at school. In only a couple of weeks he brought the gun to school trying to kidnap Lisa from school at gun point. I was assured that the school was going to back me up and press charges. But to our heartache, the principal called and told us after further conversation, Hemphill School was not going to press charges. Instead the principal went as far as to tell me that it was Lisa's word against Devin's. The school did not want to become involved. Daddy seem to catch his breath as the lawyers asked if I was the only witness to Devin pulling a gun.

Daddy quickly spoke of a phone call that came late in the hour. A boy at school had witnessed Devin pulling the gun on Lisa. He was so overwhelmed by what he witnessed that his grandmother had to rush him to the doctor. She explained how she had taken her grandson to the courthouse and filed a report, because Devin had also pointed the gun at her grandson to try and scare him away, while Lisa went to give flowers to the teacher. But instead of leaving, he hid and witnessed Devin pulling the gun. Daddy felt in his heart that he could not ask this family to become involved. Daddy did express to this woman his appreciation for the phone call.

Daddy said. "I was told by a real good friend who worked in the police department that the paper was thrown in the trash. It never made it past the front desk. It seems that the police did not consider it a serious charge."

This revelation seemed to make the lawyers take a different approach, and they didn't ask any more questions concerning the school issue.

Then they turned their focus back on me. They assured me that I had nothing to feel guilty about. Nothing I had done gave Devin the right to make an attempt on my life.

The district attorney wrote in his notebook for a moment then paused. Gently he asked, "Lisa, there is one important question that we have to ask you. Whatever the answer is, it will be okay. But we must have this information before the case goes to court. Lisa, did you and Devin ever have sex with one another?"

Though I knew that question was coming, it felt like a ton of bricks had hit me in the stomach. Unshaken, I said, "No" I followed with, "I *promise.*"

I looked at Daddy. I could tell that he was relieved at my answer. He seemed to be taking in his first breath of fresh air in weeks.

Apparently everyone in the room was relieved, and now I did not have that question hanging over my head any longer. When the lawyers completed all their questions, they said they needed to speak to the adults while I waited outside.

Lynne stood, took my arm, and walked me to the door. He whispered in my ear, "Lisa, I think there is one more person you need to talk to about your relationship with Devin." I knew Lynne was right, but I tried to talk him out of the idea. "Lisa, trust me, you were not the only one there that day. Ben needs to hear it from you before it comes out in court."

I could feel tears welling up in my eyes when I nodded in the affirmative. Lynne opened the front door for me to exit.

I walked out of the house with my feeding machine still connected to me. It was time to face my big brother. The mere thought of how disappointed Ben would be in me was overwhelming. I had always held dear our family loyalty. But now, on the inside, I felt as though I had betrayed all of them. I motioned Ben over so I could face the music. "Ben, there is something I have to tell you. But, before I do, I want you to know that I am truly sorry. If there was a way to do it, I would turn back time. I would do things differently, I promise." I cautiously began telling Ben about the depth of the relationship between Devin and me when we were alone.

To my surprise and dismay, Ben interrupted me. He informed me that he already knew about most of what I had to say. As a big brother, there were times he did some checking up on me. "I do have to know one thing, did ya'll have sex?"

The whole world seems to want to know the answer to that question, I thought. Unabashed, I looked right into my big brother's eyes and said, "No!"

A smile came across Ben's face and he said, "Good." Then he said, "Shake it off. Devin is about to go to prison, and you won't have anything to worry about." He then resumed shooting baskets. I stood there knowing deep inside my heart that I would have to win back their trust and loyalty. For evidently, I had allowed it to slip through my fingers.

THE DAY
JUSTICE PREVAILED

During my stay with Lynne, my family was nursing Mother as the doctors attempted to rebuild her arm. They had taken skin grafts and a bone graft from her leg to reconstruct her shattered arm. Everything was going well, but the details were kept from me. It was a blessing that I didn't have to wake up each morning and see Mother's arm in a sling. Lynne kept me posted on what was going on at home, but not enough to make me worry. Instead, he kept me optimistic for a speedy recovery for Mother. It disturbed me that we were getting prepared for the trial and Mother had to have a bone graft from her left leg. That would necessitate her attending the trial in a wheelchair. She would just have to swallow her pride. Mother came from a very independent family. They always said they needed no help from anyone. Now Mother was going to have to accept even more help than she ever imagined. On the inside, her emotions where raging in a silent cry for her self-preservation.

A couple of weeks passed and I was given the big news. Lynne told me that Devin's trial was scheduled. I had told everyone that would listen, especially Lynne, that I did not want to take the witness stand. The thought of having to look into Devin's eyes and testify against him seemed more than I could take. I would have to tell how our relationship had gone from a loving fairytale to an attempt on my life. Lynne had assured me that he would talk this over with Daddy and the lawyers. But he could make no promises because it was not up to him. He assured me that I would be safe in the courthouse and had nothing to fear. Hearing *that* always relaxed me to a degree, yet there was one thing I had made up my mind about. I would walk into that court room with my head held high and face Devin and his family head-on.

I wanted to be there when Mother took the stand. I felt the least I could do for my mother was support her while she undertook a hard task. It was made even more difficult because of her physical condition and mind set. I never knew my heart could beat so hard, or that every muscle in my body could feel so numb. In so many ways, I felt helpless, alone, and fragile. I was still in much pain and shock. I pleaded and begged to watch Mother testify. This was something I wanted to do so badly. I needed to face my adversary to remind him that he had failed, and I was alive, not dead!

I also begged and pleaded with the lawyers not to make me take the stand. I felt that this was beyond what I could do. My request to go to court with Mother was granted, but with a condition attached. I would have to leave with her after she testified. When I was advised of this, a part of me was excited. Another part of me trembled. I tried so hard to hide the fear from everyone. I so badly wanted my family to see me as being courageous and strong-willed.

The day finally arrived for the trial to begin. From that moment, mentally and emotionally, I entered another world in which I was on the outside of my body. I felt that I was seeing everything, but hearing nothing anyone said to me.

I did not contemplate that the ride from the house to the court house would pass so quickly. I do not remember much about leaving the car or walking into the court room. I only remember the sensation of my own blood rushing from my head down to my toes.

Taking that first step into the courtroom was a nearly impossible task. For a moment, I stood frozen. It seemed an eternity passed as I looked across the court room. I was searching for someone that I knew, a friendly face. I finally spotted a smile that I knew instantly, my dad. The look on Daddy's face almost brought tears to my eyes. In his smile I could still recognize the heartache and endless pain he had endured through the agony that his wife and daughter had experienced. The courtroom was the last place my father wanted to see us. This was a day when we all had to do our part and push past the hurt and fear.

I immediately walked toward Daddy. It appeared that he couldn't get to me fast enough. We felt all eyes were on us as we wove through the crowd and to our seats. Mother was brought in seated in a wheelchair and sat next to me. The first words out of my Father's mouth were, "Lisa, are you okay? There is nothing to be scared of."

So much of my strength was being used just to stand, and it was difficult for me to speak. I just nodded my head and tried to smile. Lynne and Bernice called me over to them a short distance away. Lynne put his arm around my shoulders and gave me a big smile. In his own way, Lynne was telling me silently that he was there if I needed anything.

Being surrounded by my family and loved ones gave me what seemed like super-human strength and made it possible for me to put one foot in front of the other.

Mother was the first to take the stand and testify. She did amazingly well.

About halfway through mother's testimony, I mustered up the nerve to look toward the defendant's table. For that brief moment, it was like my heart stopped and suddenly went numb. Every muscle in my body was tensed up and I felt as if my whole body was screaming, "Run!"

I could not see Devin's face, only his back and side. At this moment, that was enough for me. The distance between Devin and me seemed to disappear when I looked his way. It seemed as if there was no one else in the room. I did not want that feeling.

Mother's testimony came to a close, and it was time for us to exit the courtroom as gracefully as possible. To my surprise, leaving the courtroom seemed much easier than entering. We were finally headed for all the comforts of home. All the drama was behind us . . . or so I thought.

Mother and I were driven home by her friend, Chris Smith. Once there, we felt free to relax, feeling that the hard part was behind us. Although, as I sat in the living room with mother and Chris, I kept remembering what Ron, my oldest brother, had said to me in the court room. "Lisa you are our ace up our sleeve. You're like the last draw in a gun fight. We will only use you in the end if we think we need to. You will be what seals the deal on our side of the table." Those words echoed in my ears as I sat there, knowing that I might yet have to take the witness stand.

Even so, our chairs were getting comfortable, and the fact that we were in our home felt so good. I was about to relax.

But our tranquility was shattered by the phone ringing. I glanced at Mother, curious to see if she thought what I was thinking. Fear for me was reflected in Mother's eyes. I rose to my feet. I was counting each step I took as though it was my last. At my hello, I heard a familiar voice. Relieved, it was Lynne. He told me that he was coming to pick me up. I would be the last witness to take the stand for our side. I said, "Okay. Bye." I walked back in the living room where Mother and Chris were sitting and told them. I felt that I had to do it. I did not want to, but I just had to testify.

Mother immediately told me how much she wanted to go with me and to stand by my side. I reminded her that she was out-voted. Both the doctor and Daddy had said she could only make one trip. That one trip had to be for her testimony, and no more would be allowed. I tried my best to assure Mother that I could face this heart-gripping task without her. Silence filled the room as Mother pondered her situation while I waited for Lynne to arrive. These few minutes of silence gave me time to put on my game-face. I knew in my soul that I had to hold my head high. I had to walk into that courtroom and make my father proud of me. He was counting on me to carry out the most grown-up task I had ever been asked to face.

I saw Lynne as he drove into our driveway. I walked out to his car and got in. We left immediately. He reached over and held my left hand, again assuring me that I would be safe. I could not bring my self to talk, so I just nodded my head in agreement and gazed down the road. I was trying hard not to think about the moment. I dreaded having to identify Devin as the gunman.

We arrived at the courthouse, really too soon for me. There we stood, ready to enter the court house. Lynne hesitated a moment, then placed his arm around my shoulder again to remind me I wasn't going to make this journey alone, and that there were many people by my side. I took a deep breath, feeling like a condemned man walking the last mile to the executioner. At last we made it up to the top floor. To my surprise, outside the court room were cameras and reporters. Inside was a courtroom packed with people. Lynne bravely cleared a path for me to enter the courtroom. He directed me right to Daddy, who was sitting on the front row listening to the defense make their case.

I sat down on the front row listening to a witness testify. I did not like what I heard. I wasn't surprised at what Devin's family and friends said. But this witness told about what a great person Devin had always been while growing up. But what left me desolate was how Devin sat on the stand, not admitting the truth. He said that on the day of the shooting, he was just going hunting and got a little upset. He insisted that he had shot me without the intention of taking my life. He went on to claim he never pulled a gun on me at school, which only pierced my heart deeper. How he would not face up to the truth?

Stunned at his testimony, I sat there knowing that he had planned and calculated how he would end my life. Hearing Devin's voice brought me back to the front of the church, looking down a gun barrel, praying to God above to save my life. I began to feel my body going numb while waiting to take the stand. I felt as though I had only taken a couple of deep breaths when Daddy looked at me and asked, "Lisa, are you ready?" Before I could answer, Daddy reminded me that he would be right there. I had nothing to fear!

I looked at the witness stand, and then I saw the gun. It was sitting there in front of the witness stand being used as evidence. I asked Daddy, "Can they remove that gun so it doesn't have to be beside me while I testify?"

He quickly said, "No problem." Walking over to our attorney, he repeated my request. The gun was removed. Then Daddy took my hand and escorted me to the witness stand. However, he had to stop where the attorney was sitting. I, on the other hand, had to take those last few steps alone. Everyone in the courtroom was watching me as I sat down in the witness chair. I could feel holes being dug into my body as Devin glared at me. I slowly turned around and faced a packed courtroom. Frantically, I searched for Daddy. There he was, sitting as close to me as legally possible. The hurt in his eyes seemed to spill forth like water over a spillway. Then the questions came after I was sworn in "to tell the truth so help me God." I remember what Aunt Bernice had told me to do while testifying. "Face the jury so maybe they can hear you better." Each word I told the jury made me feel like I was living it all over again. I had to fight to keep from crying. However, there was something inside me that was determined not to let Devin or his family see me break down. I wanted to come across as brave and courageous, not weak like a crybaby.

I had only answered a few questions when I noticed a man in the jury acting strangely. His actions were so unusual that I stopped speaking. Then the man began shaking and then slumped out of his seat. A lady in the jury began to attend to him. Then she stood to her feet and shouted, "Does anyone know CPR?" Everyone in the courtroom rose to their feet as chaos broke out. I looked at Devin, who was staring right at me. Everyone else began to focus on the man in the jury box.

I began to fear for my safety. I called out to Daddy as once again I began to fear for my life. Daddy then walked toward me, but our attorney held him back. The judge began to hit his gavel and repeat, "Order in the courtroom." Our attorney requested that I be allowed to leave the witness stand. The judge gave me permission to step down from the witness stand, and ordered the audience to leave the courtroom immediately. Daddy rushed to my side and put his arm around me, and we began to walk out.

I noticed that the police officers finally took Devin out of the room and down the back staircase. Walking out of the courtroom, I was surrounded by my family and two undercover police officers dressed in suits and ties. We were entering the second floor staircase when I looked down the hallway. Devin was being escorted straight toward us on his way to the jailhouse. I stopped suddenly. Unfortunately, my actions made Daddy think something was wrong with me. He looked at me and asked with fear in his voice, "Lisa, are you okay? What's wrong?" I couldn't speak, so I just pointed at Devin, who was approaching us. Daddy understood without my saying a word. He understood that I was waiting for Devin to get past us. Until then I didn't want to take another step on that staircase. Devin would be passing us on the second floor. We were standing on the staircase connecting the third and second floor. Passing by us, Devin and I made eye contact. He had a sick smirk on his face. He acted as though he were untouchable. I stared right back at him with my head held high.

There, in front of my whole family, I began thinking about how my family had a history of cheating death. Now, I was going to watch justice prevail when the final verdict would come. I stood facing Devin for a couple of minutes, standing my ground. I did not do this just for my family, but for my heavenly Father as well. The scripture came to my mind that told me that he had not "given me a spirit of fear but one of love, power and a sound mind" (2 Timothy 1:7). My heavenly Father had saved my life from the attack of the enemy and had raised up my bloody, helpless, and mangled body for his honor and glory.

Devin and the police officers finally passed. Now we could continue our walk to the bottom floor of the courthouse. I was taken into a room where I waited to hear when, or if, we would be able to resume court today. We were finally advised that the man in the jury box had suffered a seizure, but he was going to be okay. Since it was almost lunch time, the judge dismissed court proceedings for lunch. This would give the man in the jury time to regain his composure. Lynne stepped into the small room. He asked Daddy if he would let me go to the Dairy Queen and get a malt with him. Daddy seemed to like the idea of my leaving the courthouse. It would be a nice break until it was time to resume court.

Lynne, Dixie, and I left the courthouse. Lynne immediately tried to cheer me up by cracking jokes. I couldn't laugh, but they did cause me to smile just a bit. We arrived at the Dairy Queen. Inside I was forced to face something that I was not in the mood to deal with at this point. Inside the Dairy Queen was Devin's family. They all glared at us as we waited to place our order. Almost immediately, Lynne saw how uncomfortable I was with these circumstances. He ordered my malt then said, "Lisa, we will leave and go somewhere else." That was music to my ears. I needed to relax as much as possible before I faced the Winchester family again. Lynne paid for my malt, and we left the Dairy Queen.

We rode around town for a while, and then drove back to the courthouse. Court resumed, and I was back on the witness stand answering questions. I looked at the jury the entire time I spoke.

Then that dreaded question came. My attorney asked me if the man who shot me was in the court room, and if so, to identify him. I knew this meant that I had to look at Devin and point him out to the jury. Looking over at him, I realized I didn't want to testify against him. My insides felt like someone was shredding them up with a knife. But I pointed Devin out and assured the jury that he was the man who had shot my mother and me.

Now it was time for the cross-examination. It was now Devin's attorney's turn to ask me questions. To my shock, he only asked a few questions. Then, to the judge, he said, "No more questions for this witness." I was pleasantly surprised. I fully expected him to call me a liar. I almost knew that he would ask me if I had led Devin on sexually. To my amazement, he didn't. This puzzled me, but at the same time I was relieved. The judge dismissed me from the witness stand and I quickly rose unsteadily to my feet. Daddy instructed Lynne to get me home as soon as possible. Part of me wanted to leave, but another part wanted to stay and hear the verdict. I wanted to hear the jury's verdict with my own ears. However, I also knew that Daddy wanted me at home. Then he could focus on the rest of the trial without distraction.

Lynne drove me home and assured me that I had done a good job on the witness stand. He then headed back to watch the end of the trial. I went inside to find Mother and Chris sitting on the couch. We all tried to talk about other things, but we all wondered how much longer the trial would last. I sat there waiting anxiously for the final verdict to be read at Devin's trial.

I found myself pacing the floor, wishing that my family would hurry up and walk through the door. I wanted to hear them tell me that it was all over. Mother seemed to be in a daze, not saying very much. She sat with both her leg and arm propped up on cushions. Knowing there was nothing she could do to ease my mind, she tried to rest. Gradually, family and loved ones began drifting into the house. Still, there was no news from the court-house. I was sitting in the living room when I saw a long line of cars and trucks pulling into the driveway. My heart took a leap for joy, realizing this must mean that it was over at last.

I didn't care who it was, but the first one through my door was going to get a barrage of questions from me. Ron, Carl, Ben, Candy, and many others walked through the front door. I stood expectantly and asked, "What did he get? What happened?"

Everyone kept quiet and allowed Daddy tell me the great news. "Lisa, they handed down a sentence of ninety-nine years."

I asked, "Daddy, why didn't they give him life?"

Daddy answered, "Lisa, we will explain everything to you later. But, just know this. He will have to serve more time with this sentence than if he had gotten life in prison." I surprised myself by allowing this bit of information to satisfy me for the moment. Then I noticed someone whom I did not recognize standing behind Daddy.

"Lisa, this is Teresa Wills. I met her at the trial. She works for the Beaumont Enterprise. She wanted to know if you would grant her an interview about the trial."

A smile crossed my face. I felt it an honor and delight to be written about in the big newspaper of our area. I shook the reporter's hand and then sat down on the loveseat in the living room. The reporter not only questioned me, but asked Daddy a lot of questions about my lifestyle. My brother, Carl, wanted to know if I was going to play basketball again. I assured them all that I would return to the basketball court. The reporter stayed long enough to catch the excitement. We were all over flowing with joy that justice had been served well in this case.

The reporter left and everyone headed for the kitchen. Our neighbor, Sue Horton, and others had brought us food to eat during this difficult time. I was hooked up to the feeding machine so that I could enjoy the food. I was sitting across from Mother in the living room. Mother refused to eat a plate of food. I really felt sorry for Mother that day. She was exhausted from the trip to the courthouse. What's more, she was groggy from the pain medication. That made her unable to really enter into our excitement. I could see that certain look in my mother's eyes. I had seen it many times as a small child. It's called compassion. I knew that there was a part of Mother's heart which could not rejoice. She could image the hurt and distress that Devin's mother was feeling right now. I sensed that she was thinking about how she would be feeling if one of her own sons was on his way to prison. These thoughts were hidden in her mind. Mother knew these were feelings she could think about but dare not express. The rest of us in the house were all rejoicing over our victory in court. We all knew that now we could sleep a lot better at night. We wouldn't be as fearful knowing Devin would be a long way from our small town, serving hard time behind prison walls.

LYNNE'S INVENTION

I still had not recovered enough to go back to my own home. I continued to stay with Lynne while trying to adjust to the unknown details concerning my health. I tried not to ask many questions, for a part of me did not want to know what lay ahead. I just tried to take one day at a time. Lynne did all that he could to put a smile on my face every day. During my stay with Lynne, my family continued to help with the rehabilitation of Mother's arm. Then, what I thought would be just another day, turned into a unique day that I will long remember.

Lynne left early that morning for the Sabine County Hospital to purchase more supplies. He had come up with an idea that I thought was nonsense. Shortly thereafter he walked through his back door. He had a wide smile on his face like a mischievous boy. I was lying on the couch watching TV. Lynne rushed through the den and said, "I found it, Lisa. Just give me a few minutes and you will be eating food again."

He went into the back room of the house and started working on his engineering project. He used some medical supplies that I had brought from the hospital. In a little while, he came back in the den carrying a funny-looking tube attached to a bubble. He had taken a blood-pressure bulb used to squeeze the cuff and attached it to some rubber tubes. He had me sit in a chair by the fireplace. Then he went to work on my g-tube and bag that were attached to the side of my neck. In short order he said, "Okay, Lisa. Now I will get you something to drink." He then handed me a glass of water and asked me to drink it. I looked down at my left side and saw what he had done. Lynne had connected the bag on the side of my neck, to the g-tube that went into my stomach.

He basically, had built me a new esophagus, but located on the outside of my body. The bulb was to squeeze, which forced the water or food into my stomach. I couldn't believe that it worked so well. I could feel water going into my stomach. My first thought was, what are the doctors going to say about this get-up that Lynne had designed? He assured me that it was okay with the doctors, and that this would be healthy for me. But I would have to remain on my regular routine of Isocal. Very soon, Lynne had me drinking away and laughing up a storm. Next, he said he wanted to test food in his invention. Amazingly, it worked; I would now be walking around with even more tubes connected to my body. I felt like some alien from outer space.

It was during this significant time that Lynne explained some things to me. He help me understand that if Devin would have gotten a life sentence in prison, it would have counted back from a certain age, making him eligible for parole at an early age. But since he was sentenced to ninety-nine years, it would be years before I had to worry about him being released from prison. My mind tried to grasp this concept while I just keep remembering what Ben said: He is going away for a long time, and you can get on with your life.

The days slowly passed by in a boring routine. One day Lynne brought good news that really brightened up my day. It was time to have the cast taken off my arm. We where driving to Nacogdoches to have the orthopedist take it off and examine my arm. That news put a spring in my step. However, I was scared deep inside that they would operate on it again. Lynne's daughter, Cindy, came for a visit that same week. She always had a way of putting a smile on my face. Cindy was going to return with us to Nacogdoches. She was attending college there, but wanted to be with us when I got the cast removed. But the night before we left, Cindy sensed that I was missing my daddy very badly. She saw that I was beginning to compare the differences between my daddy and Lynne. Then Cindy took the time to tell me something that I really appreciated. She explained that her daddy, Lynne, had a way of pushing someone hard, because he could always see the potential for success in a person. In spite of what Lynne said or did, he always had your best interest at heart. Those words helped me a lot to better understand someone that I really didn't know well. But this person had made a great sacrifice to help me through the most difficult time of my life.

Early the next morning, we drove off to Nacogdoches. Alex was going to accompany us for the trip because Cindy was going to take us for a tour on her college campus. It was fun seeing the inside of a college. I had often wondered what was on the other side of the doors. Alex and I had a good time with Cindy as Lynn and Dixie stood back, allowing us space to enjoy ourselves.

Despite the junk food, the tour of the college, and laughter with Cindy, my mind kept drifting to what the Doctor Jorgensen was going to say about my arm. Time passed slowly in a doctor's office, but finally we were in the back examining room. Doctor Jorgensen entered and immediately selected a saw and started cutting my cast off. I had not been prepared for what was going to happen once the cast was off. It only took a minute to cut the cast off. Suddenly a pain shot through my arm, which was more than I could handle. I quickly jerked my arm off the table and started crying uncontrollably. I could not understand why I was hurting so badly. Doctor Jorgensen patiently tried to explain that now that the support for my arm was gone, I could now feel the change in my arm, which was a forearm that wasn't straight and full of lead. Just when I thought I could not bear another word, Cindy was allowed in the room with me. She began consoling me. She assured me that the pain would soon go away. I should bravely hang on. Cindy had a gentle way of getting my attention and making me believe in what she was saying. She told me, "Lisa, the doctor needs to examine your arm. Please put it back on the table." I sat quietly sobbing for a few more minutes as Cindy had her hand on my shoulder. Finally the pain eased up to the point I could quit crying. Reluctantly I put my arm back on the table. The exam proved favorable for me. Doctor Jorgensen explained that all I needed next was physical therapy, and then I would be good to go.

Shortly thereafter, I went for my first appointment with the physical therapist in Hemphill. After he examined me, he explained that I could help the healing process by exercising at home a couple of times a day. Lynn's eyes sparkled with interest as the therapist showed us exercise techniques to perform at home. In no time, Lynn had a can of corn for me to place on the floor and lift it up in the air over my head. Lynn always seemed to have an uncanny way to keep my mind off the discomfort and on the goal he had set for the day. I exercised so much that even the therapist was impressed at how quickly the progress toward unfreezing my elbow occurred. In only a few weeks, I was bending my elbow and using it more and more every day. This progress helped give me the confidence that I could return home and tend to myself. While staying with Lynne, I never once got sick with pneumonia or even a cold. He protected me every way he could think of. His giving me chest therapy was critical. The chest therapy helped my lungs fight off any bacteria and kept me from getting sick.

Despite everything that Lynn and I had accomplished together as a team, I was still homesick. My heart was longing to go home. Shortly after Devin's trial, Mother's Day came, and I was spending the day with my family at the farm when I got brave enough to ask Daddy a hard question. I can still remember the look on Daddy's face when I asked if I could come back home. I sensed in Daddy's eyes that he wasn't sure if he could take care of Mother and me both. Yet behind those eyes beat a heart that could not say no. Daddy assured me I could come home that day, May 11, 1986. I was ready. Everyone in the family was concerned that my return to the neighborhood where I was shot might be more than I could handle. But my love for my family overrode any fear that I had hidden deep within my fragile body. I spent the rest of the day enjoying the company of my family. Finally at dusk, it was time for me to tell Lynne of my decision to return home. There was a part of me that did not want to tell Lynne. In these past few months, he had become far more than a dear cousin to me. When we arrived at Lynne's house, I suppose that the excitement of my decision was written all over my face. Daddy told Lynne and Dixie that I wanted to come home, and they had agreed. Lynne said he understood and hugged my neck. He invited me to come back and visit him any time, for his home would always be open to me. Daddy and I gathered up a few of my necessary things, then told Lynne that we would come for the rest later. Now in my heart, I felt one more piece of the puzzle of my shattered life was being put back in place.

Going home felt great! I so wanted my brothers to treat me like everything was normal again. The doctors had just removed the trachea tube out of my throat, so it was time to get used to the sound of my new voice. My voice was very deep and hoarse-sounding, and it would not let me speak at a high range. It only took a few days for me to begin debating with Ben about everything under the sun. No matter how hard I tried, my voice would suddenly stop working. I tried so hard to talk loudly. This made my voice squeak at first, and then no sound at all would come out. This scared me; I thought I would lose my voice for ever. Mother reminded me that the doctors warned me not to overuse my voice, and that it would take time to restore my vocal cords. This forced me to slow down on so much aggressive talking. I had to learn to be seen rather than heard all the time.

LISA BARNETT PRIDGEON

RETURNING HOME

My time at home soon began to focus on what Doctor Poke and Doctor Stein had been aiming for since January, which was a colonic interposition for esophageal replacement. The doctors said that I would eat again like everyone else one day. They planned to accomplish this by taking a part of my colon and using it for my esophagus. The doctors tried to play down this surgery to me, but something inside me told me this would be the big one. I was concerned at what really was in store for me with this operation. June finally arrived and it was time for our family reunion, which was important to me. This was going to be a special one because Lynne was going to be there. In all my years, I could not remember Lynne attending the reunion, but he was coming this year especially for me. Lynne helped me eat as we stood up in the tree house, looking down at every one eating their meal. I ate my favorite foods slowly as Lynn worked the pump and tubes he had designed. After I had finished my meal, my cousin, Jackie, reminded me of the golf cart. She had made sure that Uncle Doil had the golf cart fixed and ready for me to ride around in. All the other kids dove into the creek for a cold summertime swim in the place we all loved to gather. My family surrounded me that day with hugs and kisses, reminding me of how they had all been praying for me.

I was talking to the older members of the family when Van walked up to me and said, "Lisa, come over here for a moment." In that short moment, I learned things about my cousin Becky's husband, Van, which I had never known before. Looking into his eyes I could see how we were of kindred minds. I revealed my concerns and deep hidden fears that I had not shared with any one. Van had suffered a serious motorcycle accident that left him scarred and injured. After years of trusting the Lord and working with doctors, he was on the mend. Then looking down at the ground, he said, "Lisa, you know something? I thought for a long time that I would never have a beautiful wife because of the way I looked with my scars. Lisa, I was wrong. The Lord blessed me with Becky, who is very beautiful, and a wonderful wife. Lisa, I am going to promise you that one day a young Christian man is going to come along. You will marry him. Trust me when I say that the deep-down feeling you have that you don't deserve someone so wonderful is going to disappear. Because, Lisa, you're a beautiful young lady that will succeed in life, in whatever you set your mind to undertake." He gave me one last thought, "Lisa, look around you here. You have a large family that not only loves you, but are all praying for you." Van ended the conservation with a broad smile, and he walked away. The day was wonderful, and I tried not to think about the next day. Tomorrow we would be driving to Houston for this surgery.

THE BIG SURGERY

We left early for Houston and checked into the hospital. They wasted no time in arranging everything for the big surgery. Lynne and Aunt Bernice both came to be with me on this day, a day that they had looked forward to for months. I had much anticipation bottled up inside. Much healing and progress had been gained since the shooting. Now it was time for what seemed like the most important surgery of all, my colonic intraposition. The days leading up to the surgery had been filled with every x-ray and blood test that was possible. Everyone in the hospital really encouraged me about the surgery. They assured me that after this surgery, I would be able to eat normally again. The more encouragement they gave me, the more nervous I seemed to become. I felt that everything they were telling me was too good to believe. I had already learned from my previous stint in the hospital that when I was told, "Oh, it won't hurt, Lisa," I knew that I was in for some pain. Those words always made me grit my teeth in anticipation. My operation was scheduled for first thing next morning. I lay in the bed waiting for the 'send-off speech' from my doctors. I knew that Doctor Stein would have me laughing from the moment he walked in the door. He entered my room right before dark. His staff was with him, and within minutes he had put a smile on my face. "Are you going to be in the room with me during surgery?" I asked Doctor Stein. I knew he was not the surgeon, but his presence would help ease my overwhelming tension surrounding this operation. My heart pounded hard against my chest as Doctor Stein tried to put me at ease.

Doctor Stein, of course, had one question for me, "Alisa, what is the first thing you are going to eat after the surgery?"

I smiled broadly and replied, "Pizza!"

Everyone in the room laughed, and I was assured that I would be able to eat all the pizza I wanted. Doctor Stein ordered me to get a good night sleep because tomorrow would be a long day for me. I nodded my head, questioning inside how could I sleep tonight knowing I am going to be sliced open in the morning. I realized that my staying awake wasn't going to stop the surgery, but I could not relax my mind at all. Doctor Stein departed my room. Everyone else followed him out of the room to the hallway so they could talk in private. Their private talks only did one thing for me. They assured me that whatever was going to happen was worse than they had told me. I lay in the bed now waiting for Doctor Poke, the surgeon, to make his visit for the day. Doctor Poke was the one that I had many questions for. I wanted to know how and where he was going to cut on me. Doctor Poke finally entered my room after much anticipation on my part. Doctor Poke was not a man that smiled and laughed a lot. Instead he always held a stern look like a general in the army. Despite the serious look on his face, he looked right at Daddy and said, "Mr. Barnett I am very satisfied that we as a team of doctors have reached this point in Lisa's recovery. I believe once this surgery is complete, she will be ready to return to a normal life." I allowed him to finish his routine speech while his staff listened carefully.

At last I got my chance to speak, and I asked my questions. I was so anxious for him to hear all my questions, I spilled them all out at once. I blurted out, "Doctor Poke, where all are you going to cut me? Why are you using my colon? How long will I be in surgery? How long will I be in recovery? How many days after the surgery until I can eat?"

Doctor Poke stepped closer to the bed and replied, "Alisa, you always have questions. You will be in surgery for about eight to ten hours, and you will spend tomorrow night in recovery. Then we will take you to the ICU for a couple of days, and finally back to your room. Alisa, you will get that pizza you have been asking for soon enough, I promise." Doctor Poke paused for a moment, so I took the opportunity to ask the questions that he did not answer when he interrupted me. Doctor Poke reached down and pinched my toes that were sticking out from under the cover and said, "Alisa, don't you trust me? I want you to relax, and everything will be all right. I will see you first thing in the morning. Your job is to try and get a good night's sleep." Doctor Poke then exited the room. My family walked out into the hall way with Doctor Poke while I lay in my bed. As I gazed out the hospital window, I felt so alone and scared of what lay ahead for me. I was trying so hard to appear brave and confident about the operation. Looking out the window only reminded me that I was a long way from home in a big city. This large city seemed to sometimes overwhelm me. I wanted so much to close my eyes and make everything change. I wanted things to be back the way they were before I was shot. I longed to be sitting on our front porch back home. This was what I wished for more than anything. But, unfortunately, no matter how hard I wished or prayed, this part of my life now seemed to slowly drift by. My family soon returned and tried to make me as comfortable and relaxed as possible. But for me, no matter how hard they tried, I knew I was going to have to endure this alone. No matter what my family said to me, the fact remained that I would have to go behind those folding doors to the operating room alone. They would not be allowed to go back there and hold my hand to take the pain and anguish away. Once I went through the folding doors, it would be only the doctors and nurses to help me through the most difficult surgery I would ever face. As the night came and darkness set in, the nurse brought me my nightly medication. After taking the medicine, it was only a short while before I began to feel drowsy. I wanted so much to stay awake all night, but I soon found the medicine to be stronger than my will. As I drifted off to sleep, one question began to race through my mind—would I die on the operating table? Now no one could ever understand at that point I did not care whether or not I ever ate again, all I wanted was to live. It would not be a fun life living on a machine to eat, but I did not want to die! Up to this point, I thought I would do whatever it took to be able to eat again. But what was going to be the cost of this surgery? Scenes of movies I had seen of people dying in surgery began flashing through my mind. I finally drifted asleep only to wake at once in the night. I lay on the hospital bed with complete silence in the room. I had no idea what time I had awaken, but I knew it would not be long until they came in to get me. I stared at the ceiling while fighting tears of fear and anxiety. Each time I felt a tear about to roll down my face, I would take a deep breath and talk to myself. Ben had taught me at a young age that sometimes you just have to be your own coach during crises. At this moment, I was repeating to myself some of those positive things. *I'm going be all right, I'm not going to die, I can handle this, I'm Easual Clark's granddaughter.* I am a Barnett. *We are all fighters who will withstand until victory prevails. My Lord and Savior died that I might have life more abundant here on earth. By the blood of Jesus I will live for his honor and glory. I will live to spread the word of God all over the world. My Lord was going to heal my body while he allowed the doctors to do their part. I knew inside I was a piece of clay being molded into the image God wanted me to be, that I might be a useable vessel for God's work.* I was finally able to talk myself back to sleep for a few more hours.

I had only been awake for a short time when the nurses rolled the narrow bed into my room. I began talking to the two people who where going to push me to the holding room; from there I would wait to be escorted into the operating room. The two staff members attending to me were very nice and polite. They pretended that I was going for a simple procedure and had nothing to worry about. In an effort to take my mind off of where I was going, I asked them questions about their families and personal life. Learning about someone's family always made me feel like I was getting to know them past the professional level. Also, it helps pass the time as I was pushed down the hallways of the hospital. We arrived at the holding room where my family stood around my bed. We were all speechless. Everything that could have eased my mind had already been said, and now it was just silence. Doctor Poke and his team of doctors finally came out to greet all of us. I felt relief knowing that this was about to get underway and would soon be over. It was kind of neat seeing all the doctors I had known from my prior surgeries. I cracked a couple of jokes about two of the doctors still being single. I inquired about the rest of the team's families. The conservation was very brief as the team of doctors left. They would meet me in the operating room. No matter how light I tried to make the situation, the look on my Aunt Bernice's face told me that this was a serious operation. Lynne and Dad both had put on a faces of fatherly love that kept me from seeing their pain, but I saw instead a commitment of love and loyalty that they would be there every way possible for me. Mother's eyes were distant as if she were in another world; it seemed that reality was still too hard for her to grip completely. I was taken behind the folding doors and now could only see doctors and interns and the long narrow hallway. As they pushed me, I realized I was being taken back to the big operating room. It took only a few minutes on the operating table to prep me to be put to sleep. I asked many questions of no one in particular until I felt Doctor Poke step beside the operating table. He gave me his familiar look and told the anesthesiologist to start administering the medicine to put me asleep. The anesthesiologist told me to close my eyes and count back from one hundred. I tried my best to keep my eyes open, but I was only able to count back to ninety-six and then fell into a deep sleep.

When I awoke that afternoon in recovery room, the pain I felt surging through my body was almost unbearable. I began trying to focus my eyes because I was sure that I was still cut wide open and someone's hands were inside me. When my eyes opened, I saw Pastor Halem sitting in a chair. He helped me try to focus on where I was as I began to move around. I could feel tubes inside my left lung and stitches stretching all the way from the bottom of my rib cage to past my navel. I felt more stitches under my left breast and all over the left side of my neck. When Brother Halem got the duty nurse's attention, she came over to check on me. I had one question for her—could I have some pain medication? She told me that I had been already given some, and in a little while I would be given some more. The nurse told me that my family was anxious to see me. I wanted to see them, but I wondered what the look on their faces might tell me. To my surprise, they all had a stiff upper lip, not allowing me to think for one minute that I looked as bad as I felt. Brother Halem arrived while I was in surgery to give comfort to Mother during this time. Brother Halem was my pastor that baptized me when I was only twelve years old. He had helped me understand a lot of deeper things about the word of God. He was my pastor for about two years before he moved away. But his impression on me about spreading the gospel and living a Christian life had impacted my life in an unforgettable way. Mother had called Brother Halem at his new church and just felt she needed the support of a special Pastor during this important surgery. The next morning I was returned to my room, and Daddy was the only one now with me. Mother had gone home with Aunt Bernice. Lynne had also driven back home. They were all expecting me to be back on my feet very soon.

Only a few days had passed since my big operation. I was back in my room, but things where not going well. I could feel myself slipping in and out of what seemed like a deep incoherent state so that I was unable to respond to anyone. I could feel that Dad was getting worried as he kept pacing back and forth in my room. Finally, when Daddy could get very little response from me, he told me to hang on; he was going to get a doctor. It felt like every breath was going to be my last, as breathing had gradually grown to be nearly impossible. Daddy was out looking for a doctor when Doctor Stein came walking into my room to check on me. He had in his hand a deck of cards and wanted to show me a new card trick. However, when Doctor Stein took a good look at me, he put the cards away and took my pulse. Doctor Stein ran out of my room, and I could hear him calling for nurses and interns to get to my room immediately. I closed my eyes, frightened to open them. I was deeply concerned at what I was going to see the doctors do to me.

I kept my eyes closed until I heard Doctor Stein's voice speaking to me. "Lisa, Lisa, open your eyes and look at me." As I opened my eyes, I could see Doctor Stein standing at the foot of my bed. Nurses and interns had circled my bed. "Lisa, we must take you back to ICU for a couple of days. Right now you need to just relax because everything is going to be fine." I then noticed Doctor Stein look at Daddy who had returned to my room after looking for a doctor. Doctor Stein quickly stepped over to speak privately with Daddy. The intern began to adjust the tubes inside my left lung. Simultaneously, the nurse grabbed my right arm to start an IV. I was about to ask the intern what he was doing to me, when I felt him pull both of the tubes in my lung at the same time. Doctor Poke had left two tubes inside my left lung to drain fluid out. The pain shot through my body as though I had been shot again. I tried my hardest to scream, but I did not have enough strength or air in my lungs to do so. Tears began to steam down my face. I looked up for a brief moment and saw Daddy still standing in the door way. I could see tears welling up in my daddy's eyes and a look of anguish and heartache on his face that was almost unbearable. Daddy quickly turned to walk into the hall because he had taken all that he could bear.

The intern started talking to me to try and get my mind off of the pain I had just experienced. "Lisa, you're okay. That didn't hurt. Lisa, hang in there because everything is going to be okay," the intern assured me.

However, no matter how much they talked to me, inside I was screaming, "No, no, no, dear God, this cannot be happening!" What went wrong? I had thought just before everyone began working on me that I was either near death's door or was slipping into a coma. I was certain I was feeling too much pain not to still have life flowing through my veins. Doctor Stein told the staff working on me that there was not time to wait for a transport bed. My hospital bed could be used to transport me to ICU. They hurriedly attached the necessary machines to my bed.

As I was rolled into the hallway, I could hear Daddy saying, "Lisa, don't worry. I'm right here. I am going to ICU with you." I really could not answer anyone as they had placed an oxygen mask over my face. They were moving me quickly toward the elevators. I finally closed my eyes and tried to relax. I opened my eyes when I could hear the elevator door opening where the ICU was located. They moved me past the double doors, and we were immediately met by the ICU staff. They had already been notified that I was on my way down and to have things prepared for me. I was rushed into a private room where I was quickly lifted off my hospital bed and placed in an ICU bed. Then I was connected to more bags of medicine, fluids, and other things I could not identify. The best part of ICU then was the good effects of the oxygen. It was finally starting to reach my brain cells. I was now able to respond to all the attention I was receiving. Daddy was allowed to come and see that I had made remarkable progress.

Then Doctor Poke arrived to evaluate me and determine why I had been rushed back to ICU. Doctor Poke studied my charts for a considerable time before he made his medical opinion known. "Well, it looks like Doctor Stein was right and saved the day," said Doctor Poke. Doctor Poke was not one that liked giving Dr. Stein credit for being right about much of anything.

After a few more days in ICU, I was taken back to a regular room. Everyone was anxious for me to eat. It had been a long wait for the moment to come when I could actually eat again without tubes or machines. However, I was very hesitant to attempt my first bite. I wasn't sure that it would work, and I worried about what it was going to feel like. Finally, after much encouragement, I made an order late one evening that I wanted a hot dog with chili and cheese. The nurse said that she would get the cafeteria right on my order. It was about forty minutes before my order was brought into my room. There it was, just what I had ordered, plus a coke to drink with it. Daddy offered to cut it up for me into bite-sized pieces since one of my hands was all wrapped with an IV. After Daddy finished cutting up my food, I managed a smile and said, "Let's see what happens." I had just taken one bite when Doctor Poke walked into the room on his rounds. When he saw what I was about to do, he hurriedly said, "Oh, No!" I stopped eating. "Lisa, that hotdog has a skin that could get hung in your throat. I really want you to eat something that doesn't have a skin on it." That was all I had to hear to end my eating desire for the night. I pushed the food back and refused to eat again for the rest of the night.

My doctors kept me for a couple more weeks, and I hardly ate anything. I was finally discharged from the hospital. I was pleased to go home, but I was nervous about trying to eat. I was given one order from the doctors that I was to eat like I had never eaten before. That sounded great, but the task of eating was much easier said than done. I was hardly eating at all because I was having more trouble than I was letting anyone know about. I would take a few bites of food, then excuse myself to go throw up, but I made sure no one knew that was happening. Since I was only eating a small amount, the day would end with me being put back on the feeding machine. But the total amount I was eating had decreased, so I began losing weight. The doctors felt certain I would be able to eat, but that wasn't the case. Instead I began losing weight and feeling miserable. It came to a point that I could not even drink a glass of water without repercussions.

Mother and Daddy could see my joy for life seem to be slipping through my fingers when they had an idea. Teresa Weatherspoon was in town to visit her family, and Dad felt if I had an opportunity to talk to her, it would lift my spirits. Teresa played basketball with Candy at West Sabine and had not only went on to play college ball, but also played in the Goodwill Games. She was on her way to play in the Olympics as well. Daddy called and asked if we could come see her which to our delight she welcomed the visit. Teresa that day when we walked into her Mother's home in Pineland welcomed us with open arms. Teresa that day shared with me how her career in basketball all started and inspiration to continue playing basketball. I was barely able to hold myself up that day so weak but with my head tilted I looked at Teresa and told her my memories. Teresa said, "I can still see you coming down that court in the West Sabine gym".

"I always to told my brother Ben that you were going to the top," I said boldly. We all laughed at my memories as Teresa asked to be excused for a moment.

When she returned, her hands were full as she said, "Lisa I have some things I want you to have that I have collected. Here is a pillow they made for me at college, and here is a t-shirt I received while at the Goodwill games representing the United States. On the shirt are some pins we were given," Teresa said as she put them in my hands. I was overwhelmed with joy and so honored Pineland Hero had blessed me with such a wonderful gift. I did not leave without a picture and a joy that I had not felt in a long time. I enjoyed how Teresa reflected both on how her relationship with Christ and with her family had helped her to reach her goals in life. When we left, it made me look down deep inside, and I knew I may never play like Teresa Weatherspoon, but I had dreams and had two things she had on her side—Jesus Christ in my heart and a family that wasn't going to give up on me making it through this valley.

It was only three days till Christmas of a year that had been far greater than a few bumps in the road. My visit with Theresa Weatherspoon had helped me refocus and remember how thankful I should be about being alive. Our family had all pulled together to overcome the shooting. Now I was looking forward to Christmas at home. It would give our family the opportunity to come together and celebrate our Lord and Savior, Jesus Christ.

These thoughts were all on my mind late one evening as I watched TV in the living room with Daddy. Then the phone rang, and it was Dale, Aunt Bernice and Uncle Doil's son. Daddy spoke to him briefly and slowly walked back in the living room and called everyone together.

"There was a car wreck early today, and Steve was killed," Daddy said. I was glad I was sitting down as I curled up in a ball hearing this devastating news. Steve was our first cousin. He was Aunt Joe Neil and Uncle Ceil's youngest son. He was only sixteen years old. Sitting there, I could hear my Aunt Joe Neil screaming miles and miles away. This was their youngest child out of four, which was everyone's pride and joy. I thought, Dear God, why did I live but Steve died? I could remember him coming with his mom and dad to see me in the hospital. We talked about our unique and wonderful family and about how both of us missed Maw Maw. Steve shared how he had all the letters that I wrote to Maw Maw and how he loved reading them. I used to send her two letters a week once she moved to Bridge City nursing home. That was the last visit I had with Steve.

I was too emotional and weak to attend the funeral. Despite needing to be hooked up to a machine every three hours, I begged to attend the funeral. But Mother and Daddy insisted that I needed to stay home because I was not strong enough to sit up or stand for that length of time. Scarlet, Ron's wife, had volunteered to stay home to watch Brittany, Lee, Luke, Nelly, Angelica, and me. That day seemed to last an eternity, as I often found myself alone, crying until Scarlet would walk into the room. She would cheer me up by talking about heaven and about how we knew Steve was now with God above. She would look kindly into my eyes and say, "God has a special reason for allowing you to live. Just continue to serve and follow the straight and narrow." Scarlet spoke so confidently. I would wipe my tears and find myself laughing or talking to Brittany or Lee. These two always had a way of making me see a silver lining. The day finally came to a close as family started coming back home. But as we gathered, we were all emotionally drained. It was only by the grace of God that I was going to be able to go forward and return to the hospital and focus on my journey.

RETURNING TO HOUSTON

August found us on our way back to Houston. My doctors needed to check my progress. The three of us, Mother, Daddy, and I, were on the old beaten path to Houston. I was still being feed by the g-tube, in addition to being encouraged to eat as much as possible. During the trip, Daddy decided to stop at McDonald's and grab a bite to eat in the town of Livingston. Mother and Daddy assured me that I would be able to eat if I just took it slow and chewed my food well. We went inside to eat and relax for a little while before resuming our journey. Sitting there at the table, I enjoyed the smell and sight of the food I was about to eat. But there was another part of me that looked at the food with fear. What if my new esophagus that tasted like crap for the first few weeks did not work properly? The McNuggets smelled so good. I tried my best to muster up the courage to just pop one into my mouth. Daddy was enjoying his hamburger. I could tell that he was hungry. Meanwhile, Mother had to struggle with her hands to eat her hamburger. I slowly took one bite of my chicken nuggets. After my first bite, I quickly drank some coke hoping it would help wash it down. My plan did not work. I felt something bubbling inside my throat. Then the food rushed back into my mouth. I begun to throw up the one bite of food I had tried to eat. I quickly grabbed a napkin and put a cup in front of my mouth. I heard my daddy say, "Lisa, go to the bathroom."

I quickly stood to my feet and ran into the bathroom. When I reached the sink, I emptied a hand-full of food, coke, and phlegm into the sink; even more phlegm kept coming out of my mouth as I held my face over the sink. I wasn't sure what was happening to me. My knees begin to shake and my hands quivered trying to hold on to the lavatory. Tears began to stream down my face. All the Isocal Formula that had been fed into my g-tube earlier in the day started gushing out of my mouth and nose like a rushing river of water. What was I to do now? What were the doctors going to think?

As I washed the tears from my face with cold water from the sink, Mother walked into the restroom. Her immediate question was, "Lisa, are you okay?"

Unable to speak from the phlegm still bubbling in my throat, I just nodded my head yes. I reached up for some napkins to dry off my face as I begin to regain my composure. As I stepped away from the sink, I was overwhelmed by how much "stuff" had come out of me. We both took napkins and wiped around the lavatory so no one would have to clean the mess I had made. Mother told me that I was going to be okay, not to worry. For the life of me I could not erase that look I saw on my Daddy's face. It was a look of such hurt and bewilderment knowing there was nothing in his power he could do help his little girl. He knew that I was miserable and beyond his loving arms.

We came out of the restroom to join Daddy. I noticed Daddy had lost his appetite and pushed his hamburger to one side.

Mother dove into her hamburger again while Daddy tried to encourage me. He reminded me that we were headed back to the best doctors in Houston and I was going to be healed one way or another. Inside Daddy's eyes, I saw once again that ray of hope that God was going to take care of us. No matter how far I was down, my Daddy had a way of pointing out the silver lining in the mist of a storm. After we walked out to the car, Daddy fed me some more Isocal Formula through my g-tube. For the rest of the way to Houston, I didn't say very much. I was just wondering what the future held for me.

I had been admitted to the hospital for less than an hour when I found myself being taken back to the x-ray room. Once again it was time to start a test, which meant having to drink a special "shake" that I could see on the x-ray machine. This shake tasted like liquid cement. It didn't take long for the x-ray technician to realize that the shake would not go all the way down to my stomach. Instead, I was throwing most of it back up as fast as they brought it to me. A small amount of it passed through one drop at a time. It would go down my esophagus a short distance, then stop and begin to choke me. One would have thought doing this one time would have been enough for the doctors to examine. But, no, I drank until I thought I was going to pass out. Once drinking the shake came to an end, they began turning me around and around. It seemed that every angle possible was used to look at my esophagus. It was going to be done no mater how uncomfortable it was for me. Finally, after about two and a half hours of x-rays, I was taken back to my room.

By that evening the doctors came back to my room to explain their game plan. They explained that a small part in my esophagus was closing and not allowing food to pass through. They then discussed what was called a dilation. They felt that a few of these dilations would open my esophagus back to normal capacity. Before I could ask any questions, the doctors tried answering the questions that they had anticipated. They said the operation would be a day surgery and only last a few minutes. They assured me there would be no cutting or stitches this time around. As the doctors discussed this, I became more relaxed; I believed it wasn't that big of a deal.

Before I left the hospital, they did a dilation, which made me ask for as many grape pop sticks as they could give me. When I woke up in recovery, it felt like my throat was on fire, and I needed something cold. We finally headed home with doctor's orders to return in a couple of weeks for another dilation, which was scheduled for September ninth. That day came awfully fast. Daddy, Mother, Aunt Bernice, and I went to Houston expecting a regular day surgery of a dilation. Everything seemed to go as planned and according to normal procedure, with tubes and scopes being placed down my throat. In this procedure, Doctor Poke attempted to pass the scope into my esophagus for observation. He succeeded in doing that, but the scope would not go into my stomach for some reason. The doctors placed in the distal neo-esophagus with hopes that postoperatively it would drop down into the stomach. I was told that I tolerated the procedure well, but from the moment I awoke I knew something had gone wrong. I kept my fear trapped behind my stern "Barnett look" when I awoke. I ate a popsicle and was taken to recovery. The feeling that something was amiss on the inside didn't take long to manifest itself. I developed a very high fever and was clammy. Aunt Bernice was the first one to notice that I wasn't bouncing back as usual with my smile.

Doctor Stein came in to check on my progress since the dilation. When he read my chart and felt of my head, he quickly ordered me to be taken to x-ray room. When we entered the x-ray room, my insides felt they could go no further, but I realized that I had to do this, so I took a deep breath and cried out, "Lord, give me strength." I was going in and out of consciousness so much, I didn't recall everything that was said to me. It seemed that I lay on a cold, hard table for an eternity. Again I had to try and drink the shakes that weren't working. At long last, Doctors Poke and Stein both came into the x-ray room and gave Daddy, Mother, and Aunt Bernice the diagnosis. I was suffering from an esophageal perforation. In layman's terms, I had a hole in my esophagus that was caused by the doctor during the dilation. I definitely was not a happy camper at that point. In addition, they reported saliva had been leaking down in my lungs for the last few days. This meant I had a buildup of phlegm again, which had given me another case of pneumonia. I knew this meant more chest therapy and more breathing treatments. I was freezing on that x-ray table. I felt like an icicle, and every bone in my body was shaking. When I was taken to my room, I requested as many blankets as they could find. Aunt Bernice left after a few days, but Mother and Daddy where remaining at Texas Children Hospital for now with me. The antibiotic was reducing my fever, but my esophagus was still a problem. My doctors debated what to do about it. I felt so bad; I didn't really care what they decided to do. I not only had a hole, but I also had an esophageal stricture. The dilatation they had done on my esophagus, to expand it, had caused punctured a hole. At the same time I was still dealing with the feeling like someone was chocking me when I tried to swallow anything. I did not think this was humanly possible, but I sure felt it! When I lay down, I had to be either elevated with pillows or have the hospital bed elevated. If I was not elevated, my lungs would fill up with fluid, and I would drown in my own saliva.

The time helped pass by with visits from the Jefferson's, who had taken me in like a sheep gone astray. They would often come and pray for me when I was barely able to hold up my head. They always came with faith and encouragement that I would make it through this difficult time in my life. Despite all prayers, the days in the hospital grew tiresome, as I stared at the walls just hoping my condition would improve. Then I got a special visit from Candy. She was sitting on the couch beside my bed and Daddy had stepped out of the room for a break. She said, "I came to tell you that Jack and I have set a date for our wedding. I was wanting you to stand by the door and greet people as they sign the register book. I will also ask Jackie to stand beside you in case you need help and we will have a chair there for you in case you have to sit down." Inside my weak fragile body I felt so honored that she asked me to be a part of the wedding. I smiled and said I would love to do that for you Candy. I didn't even take a breath when I asked what was heavy on my heart, Are you and Jack going to move away because of his job. Candy, with a gentle smile on her face, explained she was marrying a hometown boy who loved Hemphill. I smiled and assured Candy I would be at the wedding which was set for September 27, 1986. I didn't know exactly how, since the wedding was less than two weeks away. I just knew my Lord and Savior could make it possible through the blood of Jesus. I asked Candy where the wedding would be held.

She replied, "At my church."

I smiled and asked, "Are we going back to Pineland?"

Candy, with love sparkling in her eyes, replied, "Yes, at First Baptist Church."

ONE LEAVES HOME

Prayers from thousands of people and love ones allowed the power of God to empower my weary body up to rise to the occasion. I weighed about 107 pounds and looked like crap, but I was happy. I was going to able to give my support and love to Candy and Jack at their wedding. I arrived home only a few days before the wedding. Family from out of town began to arrive at the Barnett castle for the wedding. Mother's arm was still in a bad way. It appeared that her mind had not refocused yet, so she was not able to help Candy very much. Daddy assured Candy that he would give her away with uttermost approval. In addition, he would gladly pay for this occasion that he had long waited for. After all, it was Candy's wedding. We all gathered that evening to witness a beautiful and breath-taking wedding. Jack was dressed in a western-cut tuxedo, while Candy was beautiful in her wedding dress. I sat there thinking that if I ever got married, I would choose some of the same colors for my bridesmaid's dresses. I also loved Candy's dress, and I desired I would get one like it some day, too. I also decided that day I would get married on Candy's birthday, just like Caroline did on mine. I was only a toddler when they got married. Caroline always told me that her wedding cake was my birthday cake! We took many pictures and then went to the reception. Lynne came up to me and asked if I was okay. I shared with him how weak I was beginning to feel. He said, "Sit here while I go talk to your daddy."

Daddy and Lynne came back over to me, and Daddy said, "Lisa, Lynne is going to take you on to the house. We won't be here much longer."

So Lynn and I left the reception just as the sun was beginning to set. While walking to Lynne's car, I looked beyond the pine trees into the distance and thought of my sister's dream. Candy had always promised me that she would one day ride into the sunset with a cowboy. Jack might have been a lot of other things, but he was indeed a cowboy. I continued gazing up at the clouds that had begun to fade away. Now I was having difficult time breathing, so I prayed silently. "Dear Lord, be with my sister in her marriage and help me to get to know my new brother!"

When Lynne and I got home, I changed clothes and all but collapsed on the couch. Lynne surprised me with a sweater he had bought for me while on his vacation. Lynne sensed that I didn't have much strength to talk with him, so he told me stories about how beautiful the Rocky Mountains were. I closed my eyes, and my imagination began running wild. I saw mountains, rivers, valleys, and deer running wild. As Lynne talked to me, I hoped that I, too, would one day see God's creation. I slowly drifted into a light sleep, but before I lost consciousness, I made a heart's cry out to the Lord that night. I dreamed and prayed that one day I would be "swept off my feet" and would marry a man of honor. I even started a list of things I wanted in a man. I desired a man of God that would protect and love me until parted by death. I drifted off into welcome slumber for a couple of hours. Then my family began arriving home, which woke me.

I will never forget the look I saw on Daddy's face when he walked through the door. I saw in his eyes the love of a father. This was a time that our family melded together, but in the midst of it all, Daddy had protection on his mind. Now he could sleep with peace at night knowing that Candy was marrying a man that would shelter her and protect her from all harm. Daddy had told me a couple of days before the wedding that he had checked Jack out in town. Daddy said all he heard people say was honorable things that made him proud to take him in as a son-in-law. Rex had reigned in our family for years as the only son-in-law. Jack was going to have a high mark to meet our expectations, but Rex had left a trail that Jack could follow when it came to understanding and providing for a Barnett daughter. The primary reason that I stayed up was to see that joy on my daddy's face. I knew that I was going to sleep well that night. I was too weak to wait for all of them to arrive. Instead I headed on to bed with my feeding machine.

I had a strange feeling after Candy moved out and across town. Not only had Dad leaned on Candy a lot to hold down things at home, but Alex, Ben, and I had turned to her many times for leadership. Although Candy had left home, she made sure that we knew she was only a whisper away. No road was too long or tree too tall to keep her away from her family. However, Candy's road from home soon became longer than I had ever wanted it to be. Jack took a job in Maine, and Candy was going with him. This was only going to be for a short time. When I heard the news, I went to Daddy for comfort. Daddy assured me that Jack was a hometown boy, and he did not think that he would stay away from Hemphill, Texas for very long. He also reminded me that no matter how far away Candy traveled, she wouldn't forget the way home.

SURPRISE, SURPRISE

I was soon to celebrate my first birthday since my life had been turned upside-down. I was far from normal, but was slowly starting to feel like my old self. I had planned to take my friend Carla to Aunt Bernice and Uncle Doil's camp that weekend. I was excited that I was going to be accompanied by Lynne and Dixie. I was looking forward to getting Carla to know my cousins Jackie, Joani, and Julie much better. There were never any dull moments at the camp when we all put our heads together. Especially when our cousins Tracy and Cristie turned up for a visit. We all had a way of laughing, joking, and playing to the tune of Uncle Doil's dancing feet. The camp was always a hideaway where we left our burden at the door. Between Aunt Bernice's good cooking and Uncle Doil's cold creek to swim in, you felt nothing but the unconditional love of God.

Little did I know what was in store for me until I walked through the door of the camp house. My family had planned a surprise birthday party. I almost jumped out of my skin when I heard the word "surprise!" I looked around and saw a crowd of people which startled me. There stood a host of my family, classmates, and friends from the neighborhood. Caroline made my day perfect by reading a poem she had written for me just before I opened the gifts. I then opened many gifts. I then saw Alex smiling like the Cheshire cat.

I stared right at him and said, "Alex, I can't believe you didn't tell me about this party."

Alex, sticking out his chest proudly replied, "I kept this a secret from even you." The room was filled with laughter and joy as I continued to open gifts. But in the background there was something I noticed; Carl had brought his girlfriend Tammy to the party. Tammy had a way of standing out in the crowd. Carl had also brought Tammy to Candy's wedding where she had stood as far from the family as possible and seemed to be watching our every move with curiosity. But now Carl had entwined her with the family while everyone made sure they spoke to this beautiful young woman that had Carl's heart in the palm of her hand.

That wonderful day soon came to a close, which took me back home. I was heavily burdened by the fact that I needed to gain weight and build up my strength. Therefore, I spent the next two months being fed with machines. I accepted everything they could pump into my stomach to help me gain weight. My imagination was working overtime, wondering what would go wrong next in my newly-formed body. But soon I had to quit thinking and pack my bags for another trip to Houston with Daddy, Mother, and Aunt Bernice. First they did more tests and x-rays to make sure I was up to the challenge. I had no idea what would happen next until that evening when the doctors walked into my room. After a short conference, the doctors left. Mother, Daddy, and Aunt Bernice were beside my bed doing their best to cheer me up. My spirits weren't very high because I knew that I still had a way to go before I was out of the woods.

Just when I thought the day would end peacefully, some interns came into my room. They all had a mischievous look on their faces, and I quickly discovered why. One of the four interns pulled a string out of his pocket and said, "Lisa, we need you to swallow this string, but leave one end hanging out of your mouth."

My first response was to laugh at this. I told them, "You've got to be joking, right?" This had to be a joke to cheer me up.

"No, Lisa, the Doctor Poke needs this inside your esophagus in order to perform the next dilation surgeries without damaging your esophagus." To my chagrin, for the next two hours a string was tied to food, candy, and other things to help me swallow the string. It did not work, for it just made me gag. After a while, the interns felt that time was running out. They needed to call the doctors and tell them they had not been successful in prepping me. I was glad to hear this because I thought there must be an easier way to accomplish the task at hand. Finally the interns left. I was so relieved. But they were gone for only few minutes, only to return with Doctor Stein. Daddy had stepped into the hallway knowing he couldn't watch any more. Aunt Bernice and Mother were wondering what would happen next. Doctor Stein then sat me up in a chair and gave me a pep talk about trusting him. He told me that I was going to have to close my eyes for this procedure and just do as he said no matter what. I pondered this for a few minutes, but I finally agreed and closed my eyes. Doctor Stein said, "Lisa, open your mouth as wide as possible." I did as he said, and before I could take a breath, I felt something big inserted into my mouth. It filled my mouth, and I quickly began chocking. Doctor Stein urged me, "Lisa, swallow, swallow. You can do it.

Swallow." My reflexes kicked in, and instinctively I tried to catch my breath by swallowing. Suddenly Doctor Stein said, "Lisa, I caught a fish. Open your eyes, Lisa." I opened my eyes and my mouth, and what I could now see was something that resembled a banana that had back-washed. I could feel something weird at the back of my throat. I looked at Doctor Stein for answers. He was holding the end of a string that I had apparently swallowed. I looked at Aunt Bernice and Mother. For the first time in years, they were speechless. Somehow I grasped the humor in all this. Here I sat in a chair with a string dangling out of my mouth like I was some bass caught on the lake.

Doctor Stein then gave orders to the interns to notify the x-ray room. Before I could get used to this weird string coming out of my mouth, I was transported to x-ray where Doctor Poke met with us. The x-ray revealed that there was something showing up in my stomach. When I asked what was on the x-ray, Doctor Stein said with a wide grin, "That was the weight you swallowed. I had hidden it inside the banana." Doctor Stein suggested we perform the dilation that night, but Doctor Poke wanted to wait until first thing in the morning. I was carried back to my room and told to try and relax. Doctor Stein also tried to make me laugh while he tied his pen to the end of the string protruding from my mouth. Then he said, "Now you won't swallow the whole string." Mother and Aunt Bernice then left for home. Dad and I planned to come home the next day after the surgical dilation.

It seemed that I would never go to sleep because my imagination was going wild. A weight in my stomach made me wonder if they knew what they where doing. Now how were they going to get this weight out of my stomach? Were they going to cut my stomach open and reach inside me to get the weight out?

When I awoke in the morning, I noticed that the string wasn't in my mouth anymore. I panicked. I located Daddy, who was lying on the hideaway bed. I yelled, "Daddy, Daddy, I ate it!" Daddy jumped to his feet to see what I was yelling about. He discovered that I had chewed the sting in half during my sleep. The string was long gone, with only a short piece tied to Doctor Stein's pen.

Daddy said, "Let me get my shoes and shirt on and I will go tell the nurse." Very soon, both Doctor Stein and Doctor Poke came to my room to see what was going on with the string. My questions were answered by another banana with a weight and string attached to the inside. Their target was my mouth again. This time I had one request, "Can I keep my eyes open?" In some strange way I knew it would help me to relax. Sure enough, he did the entire procedure again, even the trip to the x-ray room. The only difference was the surgical dilation shortly followed.

The surgery did not last long, as they had said, but they did not prepare me for how sore my throat would feel afterward. When I woke up, I had a tube coming out my nostril. It exited one nostril and was inserted back into the other one. The other end of the tube was also coming out beside my g-tube in my stomach. They told me these tubes were in place so I would not have to swallow a string every time the procedure was done. As I lay in the bed, all I could imagine was that I looked like a freak. The scars were one thing, the g-tube I could hide under my clothes, but a tube coming out one side of my nose into the other side was pushing the envelope.

I soon returned home with being told not to worry about trying to eat so much until I was through with the dilations. After a couple more dilations, phenomena, respiratory distress, and plural effusion developed in on my lungs. Unfortunately, this meant extra weeks in the hospital. Once again, I was back to receiving around-the-clock chest therapy, breathing treatments, and antibiotics. During this visit to the hospital, Daddy had to call on Aunt Bernice to stay with me due to having to take care of Mother with what her doctors where undertaking with her arm. Aunt Bernice chose to make this a rather special stay for me in the hospital by asking Jackie my cousin to come and stay with us. She was so devoted to encouraging me to get well every way possible that she gladly agreed to sleep on a sleeping bag right next to my bed. Jackie brought a video camera, and we had a blast with it, videoing everyone that came within an inch from me.

Unfortunately, I began getting worse to the point that I had five machines hooked up to me and around-the-clock therapy on my lungs. In the midst of it, Aunt Bernice tried cheering me up by getting permission for a pass to the game room. When we arrived, I had just enough strength to sit in a wheelchair. Aunt Bernice thought she would be allowed in the game room. To uttermost surprise, adults were not allowed, only the patients and their teenage friends. Aunt Bernice was nervous leaving Jackie to tend to me alone, but we both assured her we could handle things. Aunt Bernice agreed to wait right outside the door in case we needed her in any way. Jackie rolled me over to one my favorite video games, and we started playing and laughing as time slowly ticked away. We didn't know how long we had been in there, but out of nowhere weakness fell upon me. Jackie could tell by the way I was acting that we had better head back to my room. We were helped by the staff to make it back out the door, but to our surprise we didn't see Aunt Bernice. Jackie looked down to see I was bowed over and about to fall out of the wheelchair. She knelt down and asked if I knew which way to go toward my room. I directed her toward the elevators. It took all of Jackie's strength and a buck-load of determination to push me and five heavy machines. We were having a difficult time loading on the elevator when we heard that familiar voice. Aunt Bernice raced over to our rescue as she expressed how she had been looking for us and was worried half to death. We made it back to the room where nurses quickly gave me a look over and put me back on oxygen and told me to rest. The days dragged, but they slowly started turning for the better as my lungs fought to keep me alive. Despite how horrible I felt, it didn't stop them from dilating my esophagus. I found so very true the saying, "no rest for the weary." It only took a few weeks in the hospital before the doctors sent me back home. I certainly did not feel like staying in the hospital, yet I felt too weak to be going back home.

THE BOY WHO
TOUCHED MY HEART

A couple of weeks passed when Daddy and I returned to the hospital in Houston for what we thought would be just a dilation. But instead I was hospitalized again. I was told that I must gain weight, and they wanted to run more tests on my esophagus. During this hospitalization, I had some free time. I met a young boy named Matthew who would touch my heart in a special way. During the free time between my doctor's visits and x-rays, I wandered down to the playroom. This was an area on our floor where kids could go and play games or do arts and crafts. Doctors were instructed not to enter this room because they wanted the children to interact with each other. As I was walking toward the playroom, I noticed a little boy that looked to be about eight years old in a hospital bed. He had a cast from his waist down. I walked into his room and saw that the play therapy lady had her hands full with five other kids sitting at the round table playing games.

I walked up to the bed and said, "Hi, my name is Lisa. What is your name?"

"My name is Matthew," he quickly responded.

I asked him, "Hey, would you like to play with some play dough and make some cool stuff?"

A broad smile came across his face and he said, "Yeah, sounds like fun!" I walked over to the games and toys and picked up some play dough. Matthew and I pretended like we were alone in the room. We began playing with play dough and then laughed at what we where making. Matthew and I didn't talk much about anything except the game we where playing. The last thing we wanted to talk about was what lay ahead of us medically. We where having a blast, when suddenly a nicely-dressed lady walked into our playroom and started talking to the play therapist. Being a little nosey, I listened to every word I could hear, but I kept playing with Matthew. Then I realized this lady was a news reporter wanting to do a story. I didn't have time to get curious because the reporter came straight over to Matthew and me. She introduced herself and told us that she wanted to interview Matthew for a news report. Then she turned to me and said, "I would like to video Matthew and you playing together for the news report." The reporter then asked if we would like to be on TV.

Matthew and I both said yes with happy smiles on our faces. But first she had to talk to our parents and have them sign some papers. Matthew's family was just outside the playroom waiting for him, so the reporter talked to them first. Then she escorted me to my hospital room where Daddy was waiting. Our parents both thought it was a great idea and signed the papers. When

I went back to the room, I picked up a bundle of suckers that someone had sent to me and took them back to Matthew. Matthew really liked the suckers I brought back to him. Then we waited for the reporter to get the news camera set up. Matthew did a great job with the interview. After the interview, Matthew and I kept playing our game with the play dough. By the time the reporter had finished everything, it was time to leave the playroom and go back to our rooms.

I waited for the doctors to come by to see me on their rounds. After checking my chart and examining me, the doctors told me that I was looking better and had gained a couple of pounds. The best news was that in a couple of days, I should be able to go home. For the first time news about going home did not make me happy. I was hoping to stay in the hospital to see what happened to Matthew. Later that night I was watching TV in my room when I heard a knock at the door. Daddy opened the door to see a gentleman standing there whom we had never met. The man introduced himself as Matthew's father. He would like to speak to me. Daddy invited the man to come on into the room. Matthew's father walked to my side of the bed and said, "Lisa, you are all my son has been talking about today. I went to an Astro's baseball game last night and got Matthew's favorite player to autograph this t-shirt I had bought for him. When I brought it to him tonight, he said he wanted you to have it."

My mouth fell open in shock. I was speechless. I wondered how Matthew could give up such a souvenir as this to me. Matthew's father handed me the t-shirt, and I reluctantly accepted it. I saw that Daddy looked just as surprised as I was about this most honored gift. Matthew's father informed Daddy and me that Matthew was going to have surgery the next day. He didn't give many details, but just knowing that Matthew was going to have a very important surgery made my heart feel so heavy for him.

I had to wait until the next morning to thank Matthew for the gift he had sent, because he had already gone to sleep for the night. I could hardly wait for daylight to come; I wanted so much to spend some time with Matthew. When I finally woke the next morning, I hurriedly dressed and waited for the nurses to make their morning rounds. To my surprise, the doctors came in that morning and told me that I was being discharged that day. My first thought was, "Oh no, I can't leave yet," because I want to spend more time with Matthew. While the nurse and doctors were making preparation for me to leave, I finally found some free time to slip away. I told Daddy that I wanted to go see Matthew. Daddy said that was okay. I walked down the hall to Matthew's room and saw that he was not in his bed. Then I remembered the time he was scheduled for surgery. I found a clock at the nurse's station and saw that it wasn't yet time for the surgery. I asked the nurses where Matthew had gone. The nurse didn't want to tell me anything, but I persisted. I explained to them that I had to thank him for my present. One of the nurses finally informed me that Matthew had already been taken down to the holding room awaiting his surgery. I thanked her and rushed back to my room to talk to Daddy. There I met some nurses who were looking for me. It was time to take my vital signs because I was about to have a breathing treatment.

Afterward I asked Daddy if he would take me down to the surgery floor so I could talk to Matthew's family. Daddy said, "That's fine. I must go tell the nurses we will be gone for a little while." After Daddy returned he had to lead the way. I had no idea which way it was to the surgery floor. I had always been taken there on a bed with people surrounding me, so I could not tell which direction we took. When we reached the surgery floor, we went into the waiting room. We saw Matthew's father and mother sitting there. I walked to them and asked, "Is Matthew already in the surgery room?" His mother told me that they had just taken Matthew back and it was going to be a long surgery. Daddy and I sat down beside Matthew's parents. I sat right beside Matthew's mother, whom I had met already the day of the TV report. As I sat there, I could feel the pain and anguish his mother was feeling as she waited for a report from a doctor. Both of us fought to keep from crying as we talked about how special Matthew was to everyone he had ever met. For a brief moment, his mother and I were unable to speak as our hearts bled for Matthew. Inwardly, I asked the Lord why I was there. He revealed to me that I was to pray for Matthew with his mother and to pray a prayer of faith. I almost choked at the thought of praying aloud in a public place, but the Holy Spirit kept burning inside of me like a wild fire. I took a deep breath and said, "Mrs. Martinez, is it okay if I pray for Matthew with you?"

She quickly responded, "Yes, we need all the prayer we can get."

I offered a short prayer requesting the Lord to intervene on Matthew's behalf so that the surgery would be successful. I desperately wanted to see Matthew walk. After I prayed, Daddy and I went back to my room to wait to be released from the hospital. Shortly before we left for home, we learned that Matthew was out of surgery and had returned to his room. I stopped by to see him, but he was sound asleep. I left concerned about Matthew's condition and about what his family was going through. He was so young to be going through this kind of surgery.

ONE LAST TIME

Returning home didn't stop the frequent visits for dilation about every few weeks. Finally Doctor Poke wanted to run some more tests, so he hospitalized me. Mother and Daddy both went with me to the hospital, but when Daddy saw that a serious decision had to be made, he sent Mother back home. After another dilation and more tests, Doctor Poke came to my room late one evening. He wanted to advise us just where we stood with my healing. Doctor Poke explained that I needed another operation where they would cut me open again. I simply curled up in a fetal position like a little baby, shaking my head no. Daddy spoke up at this point and explained that he would allow me to make this decision. It was the first time that I had any say in whether or not I went to surgery. Lying in that hospital bed, it felt like the world was crashing down around me. The mere thought of being on a feeding machine the rest of my life seemed like an unbearable thing, but if it were left up to me, there would be no more surgeries. My insides where screaming, "We can't take any more."

Daddy looked at me in the bed and asked the difficult question. "Lisa, do you want to have a surgery where they cut into your esophagus and repair it?"

I wanted so much to respond yes in order to make Daddy happy. But this time I said a hearty no. I felt that this answer needed an explanation. I explained that my God of gods could and would heal my esophagus, and I wouldn't need surgery.

"Lisa," Doctor Poke quickly said as he reached down and touched my toes, "I don't want you to ever think that I go into the operation room without God on my side. I always look to him for direction and guidance when I am in surgery. Please, Lisa, reconsider so I can fix your esophagus this time." Those words made a deep impression on my heart. I now saw my doctor as a Christian man, giving God the glory he deserved. But I was going to be stubborn and hold to my decision. Daddy kept his word and left it up to me. He said nothing as he escorted Doctor Poke out of the room. They talked in the hallway outside my room, and I couldn't hold back the tears any longer. I rolled over on my side and began to cry out to my heavenly Father. There seemed to be a part of me that didn't want to see another sunrise. I felt numb inside, as though I could not walk another step down this path. I cried out for the Lord to make me strong and give me courage to face the days ahead. I pleaded for him to heal my wounded and frail body.

Daddy and I returned home the next day, and word quickly spread through the family about my decision. Mother, of course, was worried about me and not really sure how to support me in my decision. She needed to talk to Caroline about this. Caroline took this opportunity to remind Mother what she had always taught her children about healing. Mother had raised us kids on the anointing oil in a bottle that sat on the fireplace mantle. The only medication allowed to stay in the house was a bottle of aspirin that would last the whole family three years at a time. Mother no matter what we came down with she would put the oil on our foreheads and prayed for the Lord to heal us. My Mother had stood on James 5: 14 and 15; Is any sick among you? Let him call for the elders of the church: and let them pray over him anointing him with oil in the name of the Lord. And the prayer of faith shall save the sick, and the Lord shall raise him up…. Caroline said Mother you taught us all to have faith and trust God to lead us and guide into all truths. You have always told Lisa that through Christ Jesus and his blood that all things are possible. She has been through a lot Mother now we have to trust God to take care of Lisa. Remember Mother the faith Lisa has right now is because of what we as a family has stood on as a God fearing family. But most importantly, Caroline told Mother how she understood that I had to have a break from the operations. After talking to Caroline, Mother seemed more understanding of my position. By this time in my life, I had undergone numerous operations within eighteen months. But in the midst of this, I tried not to think about how worried my daddy was about the situation. He understood that just keeping my head above water seemed to be all I could bear at this time.

The nights, with few exceptions, became a nightmare that I tried to keep hidden from everyone. After the doctors stopped the dilations, for some reason I found it very difficult to sleep. Every night, after I was sure everyone was asleep, found me gathering up the pillows and cushions out of the couch. I found it necessary to prop myself up so I was elevated as much as possible. There were several times that I almost drowned in my own salvia as I was propped up in bed trying to sleep.

I would catch myself gagging, then coughing in an effort to clear my airway. Every night seemed to get more difficult for me. I was careful to put the pillows and cushions back in their place before anyone got up in the morning. But as the days slowly dragged by, the problem grew worse. It got to the point that I would have a puddle of salvia running out of my mouth on to the floor. Finally, after four long, drawn-out months, I was exhausted and overwhelmed with distress. Mother came into my room early one morning to check on me. When she saw me trying to clean up my mess with rolls of toilet paper, she wanted to know what had happened. I wanted to simply disappear as though nothing had ever happen. I was unable to speak as Mother kept asking questions. My night shirt was completely wet from salvia that had drained on to the bed. Mother finally got me to reveal the secret that I had tried my best to keep hidden from everyone. Mother was very quiet for a couple of minutes. I could tell she was asking the Lord what to say. Mother then sat beside me on the edge of the bed and said, "Lisa, God sometimes uses doctors to bring our healing to pass. Have you asked the Lord what he wants you to do about the surgery?"

I responded, "No, I just thought God always wanted to heal me."

Mother had a quick answer, "Yes he does Lisa, but God placed doctors here for a reason. We should not be so stubborn that we will not take a blessing of God from a doctor." Mother continued, "Here, Lisa, I will clean this mess up. You go on into the bathroom and clean yourself up. Think about what I said and pray about it."

I cleaned myself up and returned to my room to ask God what he wanted me to do about the surgery. A peace came over me as though a dove had landed on my shoulder. I felt the Lord leading me to agree to one last surgery. After I finished dressing, I walked out of my bedroom and saw Daddy in his recliner. I asked Dad a pointed question, "Dad, if you can call Doctor Poke today, and the hospital can take me, I will have the surgery. But I will not wait for a week or more to be checked in the hospital."

I could see an immediate relief come over Daddy. It had been a long time coming. Daddy happily replied, "Go on to school, Lisa. As soon as Doctor Poke gets to his office, I will call him." Daddy said, "Lisa, I think you are doing the right thing." Daddy had this look of approval on his face that he gave us kids when we had made a decision that made him proud.

As I left for school I told Mother, "Please call the school and give me a message when Dad talks to the doctor." Mother assured me she would call me as soon as she knew something definite.

I was in algebra class when I received a note from the office. Eagerly I opened the note. I read that we were going to Houston first thing in the morning. My heart skipped a beat. I had to take a deep breath. After the class was over, I found myself sitting alone near the old gym. I really did not want to go to my last class.

I was about to start crying when Lisa Lynn White noticed that I was upset about something. She came over to me and asked, "Lisa, what is wrong with you?" I told her I had just found out that I must have another surgery. Lisa then put her hand on my shoulder and said, "Lisa, I will be praying for you myself. I will also ask my whole church to pray. I know it won't be easy, but God is going to take care of you." Those few words of encouragement helped me to keep from crying. They were like a ray of sunshine of hope in the midst of a storm. I was able to pull myself together and make it through the rest of the day.

When I got home that afternoon, Mother explained that Doctor Stein was out of the country and would not be back for a couple of weeks. She was afraid that I would be upset at the news. Although those words where hard to hear, I knew it was time to get this surgery over with as soon as possible. That night I didn't really sleep. I just sat up in my bed staring into the darkness.

Morning came very slowly. I told Alex and Ben goodbye even before the sun had risen. Saying my goodbyes to them made me choke up. Somehow it seemed that this was my final goodbye. But I lost that thought when Ben looked at me and said, "See you when you get back." Soon, Daddy, Mother, and I headed off to Houston. Candy, of course, would look after Alex and Ben.

THE SCALPEL CUTS AWAY

It seemed to take forever to check into the hospital that time. We were barely in our room when Doctor Poke came in. For the fist time, I saw a joy and happiness on his face that I had never seen before. He said to me, "Lisa, we have come too far to quit now. I am so glad you agreed to the surgery. I am positive that it is going to work, and you will be able to eat normally again. I have scheduled the surgery for first thing in the morning. This one will only be about three hours. Just get a good nights sleep, and I will see you first thing in the morning." Doctor Poke then gave me a shot to help me relax. I had the bed propped all the way up, and I was able to sleep despite salvia running out the side of my mouth.

Lynne, Dixie, and Aunt Bernice had all driven down for the surgery. Just when I was getting settled in, Aunt Bernice had to unexpectedly leave and return home. Aunt Bernice received a phone call that her brother-law had a sudden heartache and died. She knew her sister would need her shoulder to lean on.

Aunt Bernice had to leave, but she reminded us that her heart wanted to be two places at once under the circumstances.

But just when we thought plans would go as scheduled, we were all in for a surprise. Unfortunately, the assistant surgery that was brought in on my case misunderstood everything Doctor Poke was excepting from him. Once I was in the surgery room, the surgeons found out they were not on the same page. Therefore my surgery was postponed for three days. The assistant wanted more time to become more familiar with my past medical records and schedule more time in the operating room for me to be under the knife. Lynne and Dixie had other obligations and had to return home. Three more long days rolled by with me just taking time to visit the playrooms in the hospital. But finally the big day came I handled the surgery rather well, and waking up was much easer this time. This time I noticed that there were no tubes coming out of my lungs. Also, I wasn't cut down my chest and stomach as usual. After recovery and spending a few nights in ICU, I was back in my room. Doctor Poke said to wait three days before trying to eat. Three days slowly passed and finally it was time for another food showdown. I felt more confident when I started eating. As I chewed a bite of food, I felt as though things where going to work right. Sure enough, the food went all the way down. Daddy was overwhelmed with joy. I could not leave the hospital until I was eating better. Unfortunately, Doctor Poke wanted the g-tube to stay in until I had adjusted to eating normally.

I was finally able to eat normally again after returning home. I was still rather cautious, but it sure felt great eating with the family. My stitches were soon removed and the doctors said they would schedule me to have the g-tube removed. Around two months passed by. By this time I was improving and healing rapidly. It was now time to schedule the procedure to have my g-tube removed. As we were leaving for the hospital, Mother asked me, "Lisa, do you have Matthew's phone number? If so, maybe we can call him while we are down there and see how he is doing." Mother and I where staying in the hospital for a few days. Doctor Poke wanted to run more tests to see just how well I was doing. Daddy had to go back home to take care of some business. It was on my second day in the hospital when the doctors performed a surgical procedure to remove my g-tube. Then mother called the Matthew's family.

The next night, there was a knock on my hospital door at about six-thirty. Mother opened the door, and there in a wheelchair were Matthew and his father. I said, "Hey, Matthew."

The first words out of his mouth were, "Lisa, I can walk now." He looked up at his dad and asked permission to show me. His daddy agreed and Matthew stood. Without any assistance, he walked over to my bed.

I said, "That's great, Matthew. Before long you'll be running around your house at full speed."

Matthew sat back down in his wheelchair. We talked for over two and a half hours. He was a special friend that made all my visits to Texas Children seem worth the effort. Just seeing the Lord's working in his life reminded that I served a mighty and loving God. Since they had a seventy-mile drive, they had to leave quite soon.

After Matthew left, I closed my eyes and prayed that God would become more real to Matthew as he grew up. I prayed that he would be a mighty man of God and witness to everyone he met. I had a troubling feeling that I would never see Matthew again. I had an inner voice telling me to enjoy the moment, because it would have to last me a lifetime. I would remember him as that young boy who touched a special place in my heart when I was going through a hard time in my life. Matthew had reminded me just how much I loved my niece and nephew, Brittany and Lee. They were only a few years younger than Alex and I, and we grew up together. There wasn't anything that Ben, Alex, and I would get into without including Lee and Brittany. I lay in bed that night hoping that Lee and Brittany would always remember the days we shared before I was shot. The days when I could run without coughing and eat Thanksgiving dinner without a machine were special.

AFTERWORD

When I came home, everyone was happy to see that I no longer had tubes coming out of me. It was time to start living again, yet I knew I would never be the same. I would now cherish every breath of life as though there were no tomorrow. I have purposed that with God's help, this tragedy will be for His glory, and I strive daily to become stronger and closer to Him. I will not live a life of bitterness and anger. Instead, it will make me a better person. I would daily in my heart choose to forgive and replace hate with laughter and joy of the Lord. I cried out to my Heavenly Father above when the memories of what happened overwhelmed me. I cried out for souls to be saved, people healed, and lives forever touched as the truth prevailed for God's honor and glory. My Lord sent his son Jesus to die on the cross. It was the shedding of His innocent blood that makes a way for the sinner. We are promised eternal life when we accept His free pardon for sin. My blood being spilt on the ground that day is a constant reminder of the sacrifice that Jesus made when He shed his blood for sin. I claim the victory that is available to all—victory over sin by confessing that He is Lord and asking His forgiveness and accepting Him as savior.